ACHIEVING MONETARY UNION IN EUROPE

SAGE Publications

Prepared by the
National Institute of Economic and Social Research for the
Association for the Monetary Union of Europe

The Association for the Monetary Union of Europe (AUME) was set up in 1987 as a voice of Europe's business community, expressing the need for monetary stability and a single European currency. It does so by taking public positions on matters related to European Monetary Union in the European media. It is conducting research in order to clarify some of the issues in the public debate. The Association also organises seminars and publishes material in order to improve knowledge of EMU and the practical use of the ecu.

The National Institute of Economic and Social Research (NIESR) is an independent non-profit-making body whose object is to increase knowledge of the social and economic conditions of contemporary society. It conducts and publishes research by its own staff and in cooperation with the universities and other academic bodies.

ACHIEVING MONETARY UNION IN EUROPE

by

Andrew Britton and David Mayes

SAGE Publications

Prepared by the
National Institute of Economic and Social Research for the
Association for the Monetary Union of Europe

© National Institute of Economic and Social Research 1992

First published 1992

All rights reserved. No part of this publication may be reproduced, stored in a retrieval system, transmitted or utilized in any form or by any means, electronic, mechanical, photocopying, recording or otherwise, without permission in writing from the Publishers.

SAGE Publications Ltd
6 Bonhill Street
London EC2A 4PU

SAGE Publications Inc
2455 Teller Road
Newbury Park, California 91320

SAGE Publications India Pvt Ltd
32, M-Block Market
Greater Kailash – I
New Delhi 110 048

ISBN 0-8039-8718-8
ISBN 0-8039-8719-6 pbk

Printed in Great Britain by Billing and Sons Ltd, Worcester

Contents

Preface viii

Summary ix

1 **The road to monetary union** 1
    The postwar international economic order
    Integration in Europe
    The precursor to Maastricht in the 1970s
    The European Monetary System
    Closer European integration
    The economic transformation of the Community
    The basis for Maastricht

2 **The Maastricht Treaty on EMU** 22
    The main provisions
        Stage 3
        The form of the ECSB and the constitution of the ECB
        Economic policy
        Other aspects of the Maastricht Treaty directly impinging on monetary union
    The nature of the new treaty and the compromises it involves
        The need to compromise
        The aims and accountability of the ECB
        The process of transition
        The extent of economic union required
        The need for social and economic cohesion

3 Economic and monetary policy in a United Europe   38
Price stability
Monetary policy
 The exchange rate of the ecu
Fiscal policy in an EMU
Reactions to shocks

4 Achieving and maintaining convergence   50
Nominal convergence
Maintaining convergence
Wage and price flexibility
The role of national governments
Fiscal policy in member states
Restoring full employment
Structural convergence
Conclusion

5 Cohesion and economic and monetary union   63
The importance of cohesion and real convergence as a precondition for monetary union
What can the Community's policy achieve for cohesion
The budgetary perspective for 1993-8
Further measures
Concluding remark

6 Broadening the Community   79
EFTA and monetary union
A southwards expansion?
Eastern and central Europe, a major problem and an opportunity for the ecu
Broadening and deepening

7 The member states   92
Germany
France
Italy
The United Kingdom
Spain
The Netherlands
Belgium and Luxembourg
Denmark

Greece
Portugal
Ireland
Conclusions

8 Microeconomic conditions for monetary union   **126**
The immediate microeconomic considerations from monetary union
The wider framework of change
Implementing the single currency

9 The timetable   **135**
Achieving the timetable
A partial EMU
Concluding remark

References   **143**

Preface

The Treaty on European Union was signed at Maastricht on 7 February, 1992. No-one who reads the text of that Treaty can fail to be impressed by the magnitude of the decision which has been taken and the importance of its implications for the future of Europe. In the course of this year the Treaty needs to be ratified by each member state. As a result it will be extensively discussed in each member state, both its grand design and its fine detail. This book is our contribution to that debate insofar as it concerns economic and monetary union. It is addressed to policymakers, to the business community, to economists and to the general public. We are concerned to set out what needs to be done in order to achieve monetary union in Europe.

The book was written in the early months of this year, but it arises out of a programme of research undertaken at NIESR in the course of 1991 with the support of the AUME. The results of that research, and parallel work by our colleagues in Germany, France, Italy, the Netherlands and Spain, were presented to a conference immediately after the Maastricht Summit in December. The papers from that conference are published as 'Economic Convergence and Monetary Union in Europe' edited by Ray Barrell.

We are grateful to the AUME for their support of our work in preparing this book, and in particular to Stefan Collignon for his help and encouragement. This continues an association which began in 1990 when we worked together on 'A Strategy for the ECU'. It is gratifying to see that the programme adopted at Maastricht does not differ very greatly from the strategy advocated in that report.

We are also grateful to the members of staff at the Institute who helped us write this book, especially to Frances Robinson who prepared the text for the publisher.

Summary

The road to monetary union

Economic and monetary union will fulfill an aspiration which was formed more than forty years ago. It will bring together the political vision of a more united Europe with the economic ideal of monetary stability. The Treaty is not, of course, the final destination, but it makes possible the achievement of EMU by the end of this decade. Experience of EMU will then make yet closer integration possible, and even necessary.

In the 1970s public opinion was not ready to accept the discipline required for price stability, and member states still hoped that they could solve their economic problems on their own. The situation in the 1990s is very different and much more favourable to the venture of EMU. The successful operation of the European Monetary System and the implementation of the Single Market programme provide a secure foundation on which EMU can now be built.

The Maastricht Treaty

The text of the Treaty demonstrates the determination of member states to reach agreement on a range of very complex issues; it naturally reflects a compromise between the rather different perspectives brought to the subject of EMU by governments with different shades of political colour and states with different economic interests.

One of the most striking features of the Treaty is the emphasis on price stability, and the responsibility of the European central banking system for its achievement and maintenance. After decades of persistent inflation this is an aim which can be endorsed by popular opinion in all member states. The constitution of the central banking system is designed to provide the independence from political pressure which is recognised as essential to the pursuit of this goal.

The Treaty lays down in some detail the process of transition to EMU. This involves the fixing of exchange rates and the creation of new institutions. There is a timetable with 1997 as the earliest date for the implementation of EMU, and 1999 as the latest. This will be followed by the replacement of existing currencies by a single European currency, the ecu. There are also precisely defined convergence criteria which shall be used to judge which member states are ready to participate in EMU when it is set up. These criteria cover relative rates of inflation, exchange rate stability, the debts and the borrowing of governments and relative rates of interest.

In parallel with EMU, the Treaty advances the process of political union, providing the framework for joint decision-making essential to the success of economic policy.

Policymaking in a United Europe

Once EMU is well established, the achievement of very low rates of inflation by Germany, France and some of the member states in the late 1980s will be extended to all states that participate in EMU. There will be a single currency and one monetary policy set by the European central bank. Interest rates on similar assets will be the same in all member states, and short-term rates will be under the control of the central bank. There will be a Europe-wide definition of the money supply for which the central bank will set a target.

The ecu will be an equal partner in a tri-polar international monetary system with the dollar and the yen. Policy coordination with America and Japan will be mainly a matter of cooperation between central banks. It will not be possible to pursue an exchange-rate policy for the ecu which is not consistent with the aim of price stability in Europe to which the European central bank will be committed.

Economic policy will from time to time have to react to shocks, either originating in Europe or outside. The central bankers will be well aware of the need to tighten monetary policy in response to an inflationary shock, for example a rise in world commodity prices. They will stand ready to respond in an appropriate way to a deflationary shock, for example a financial crisis in world markets. In that case the danger to be averted would be recession and high unemployment rather than inflation.

Achieving and Maintaining Convergence

EMU will only work well if it has the support of the governments in member states, who will each be answerable for price stability and economic prosperity to its own electorate. Rates of inflation in all participating states must be similar, if not identical. Balance between member states will be maintained by the adjustment of relative costs and prices, a process which requires the right kind of flexibility in labour markets as well as the markets for goods and services. However, some measures of direct intervention will also be required as exemplified by the Community's structural policy.

The scope for demand management by individual member states will be limited. They may find it helpful to increase the 'built-in stability' of their taxation and public spending systems - that is, the degree to which government borrowing rises and falls automatically with the cycle of economic activity as taxes rise and social security spending falls in line with the rate of economic growth. The restoration of full employment will depend on better national policies towards training and labour mobility, as well as on extinguishing the inflationary psychology which still prevails in some member states.

The process of convergence should not stop when EMU has been formed. For EMU to work well there should be a continuing process of structural convergence, so that the institutions of member states become more compatible with one another. Consider the response to a rise in European interest rates: if institutions and economic structures are very different in different member states there could be very little response in some countries, but widespread bankruptcy or unemployment in others. The process of structural convergence will gradually remove discrepancies of this kind.

Cohesion and EMU

It is generally accepted that there will be a substantial net benefit to the Community but this does not stop there being considerable short-run costs for some regions. Some of the member states which have furthest to go in meeting the convergence criteria of the Treaty, also have regimes with some of the lowest levels of income per head. Thus the issues of convergence and cohesion, although they are quite distinct in economic theory, tend to be linked together in political practice. If the transition to EMU is to succeed, all the member states need to feel that they are getting something out of the move to European Union. The deal which was struck at Maastricht included the establishment of a new cohesion fund.

The limit to the size of the Community budget severely restricts what can be done to even out income levels between member states. This constraint would be eased if the CAP were reformed (without causing major problems in rural areas), and if funds could be transferred to other programmes which have more of an equalising impact across member states. The funds which are specifically allocated to the objective of cohesion could be used more effectively to raise the living standards of the poorest people in Europe.

Broadening the Community

The transition to EMU will take place in parallel with the enlargement of the Community and with the development of new relationships with the countries of the east. It is sometimes suggested that the processes of widening and deepening will conflict with one another; on the contrary, the timing is such that the two can go forward in harmony.

The present member states of EFTA could all take their place in an EMU with no more difficulty than the existing members of the EC. Some, Austria for example, would find the transition to EMU very easy indeed. Negotiations could be conducted speedily so that some of the new members of the Community can join EMU from the start.

The situation of the countries of eastern and central Europe is clearly very different. The timescale for their membership of the Community, if they apply, will be longer than that of the transition to EMU. There is a case for creating an ecu zone within which they could progress towards the establishment of a free market system, with various degrees of attachment to the European Union. It is possible that their integration will be a step-by-step process, so that for some time they are members of the European Union without participating in EMU. Some of the present members of the EC may also be in that position for some years.

The present member states

Member states have already made substantial progress towards convergence, which may act as a spur to others, but in some cases there is much that still needs to be done.

Germany

EMU is impossible without German participation. What is more in doubt is the attitude that the German government will take to the timetable and the initial membership. If price stability is not achieved in Germany itself then German opinion may favour delay and the exclusion of any member state on the borderline of convergence. If the assimilation of the eastern länder proves difficult, then German opinion may opt for a narrow version of EMU so as to limit competition with its own 'developing economy'.

France

The wish of the French government, naturally enough, is to take part in the decisions which shape the monetary policy of Europe, not just to follow a German lead. Hence the French wish to push ahead rapidly from EMS to EMU. Earlier attempts at monetary union in the 1970s foundered because the French and German economies still responded so differently to shocks. The degree of integration has now increased and the risk is much less. The French have achieved convergence and, if that was all that was necessary, EMU could go ahead now.

Italy
The participation of Italy in EMU from the start is still uncertain. The criterion for government debt has been drawn up in such a way that Italy will have great difficulty in meeting it, and member states collectively will have to pass judgement on the Italian case. If the decision were to be taken today Italy would probably be excluded, but provided that the rate of inflation is substantially reduced in the next few years a more generous treatment might be expected when the day of reckoning comes.

The United Kingdom
Britain has been a late entrant to the Community and also to the exchange-rate mechanism. The option could be used to be a late entrant to EMU as well, but opinion is shifting in favour of playing a more central role in the development of Europe. For the British economy the transition to EMU is not easy. The rate of inflation is now low, thanks to the recession, but in the past the economy has been very inflation-prone and it remains to be seen whether old habits have been broken.

Spain
The Spanish economy is in the process of rapid structure change and development, bringing it into line with other countries of Europe. Perhaps for that reason unemployment has been, and remains, relatively high. To meet the convergence criteria growth will have to be restrained so that inflation falls and the fiscal position is strengthened. It would be a strange outcome if Spain, a very recent member of the EC, were to be accepted into EMU whilst Italy, a founder member, was rejected. So far as the simple arithmetic is concerned that could easily happen. In political terms it is less easy to contemplate.

The Netherlands
In many respects, the Netherlands is already in a monetary union with Germany. It is hard to imagine EMU taking place without the Dutch. But for this to happen the debt criterion may have to be interpreted in a relatively relaxed way. The level of long-term interest rates on public sector debt suggests that the markets regard the Netherlands position as satisfactory.

Belgium and Luxembourg
For Belgium also there is a problem of debt. It is unlikely that the criterion in the Treaty could be met within the likely timescale for EMU. On other grounds however Belgium and Luxembourg would be model members and the convergence of interest rates shows the confidence that the market has in them.

Denmark

If the Danish economy maintains its recent performance it should have little difficulty in passing the entrance examination for EMU. Indeed the example of Denmark will probably be held up as the right one for Sweden and Norway to follow if they too want to joint the Community. But the Danish experience includes a high rate of unemployment which the other Scandinavian countries still hope to avoid.

Greece

There seems little chance of Greece meeting the convergence criteria either for debt or for inflation unless there is a major and fundamental change in fiscal and monetary policy.

Portugal

It is the intention of the Portuguese government that the escudo should join the exchange-rate mechanism as soon as possible, and a determined attempt is promised to prepare for participation in EMU at the first opportunity. The level of borrowing may not be unreasonable for a developing economy, but inflation is likely to be a problem as well.

Ireland

The recent performance of the Irish economy is impressive and Ireland must be a serious candidate for participation in EMU from the start. But the level of unemployment remains very high.

Micreoconomic conditions for EMU

The full benefits of monetary union will only arrive when the ecu becomes the single currency of Europe. The Treaty does not settle the issue of when this most important step will be taken, whether it is simultaneous with the beginning of EMU or soon afterwards. Delay should be minimised, but firms need considerable notice in advance of the changeover. This highlights the need for as clear a timetable for EMU as possible.

The timetable

Some dates can already be written into the diary for future years. Following ratification the Treaty takes effect on 1 January, 1993. A year later on 1 January, 1994, Stage 2 begins. By the end of 1996 a decision is taken on whether Stage 3 goes ahead, with 1 January, 1997, as the earliest starting date if a majority of the member states have converged. Failing that, by 1 July, 1998, a decision must be taken as to who will qualify to participate in EMU, which must begin by 1 January, 1999, at the latest.

It is unfortunate that the timetable allows for so much uncertainty as to the starting date and the participants in EMU. We have tried to clarify the situation as much as we can, so as to help those who must now make plans that depend on the outcome. In doing this we have to make political as well as economic judgements.

We expect EMU to begin on 1 January, 1997, the first opportunity. The following member states are almost certain to participate from the start: Germany, France, the Netherlands, Belgium, Luxembourg, Denmark, Ireland and Austria (assuming it is by then a member of the European Union). The following member states are very likely to participate from the start: Italy, the United Kingdom, Spain and Sweden (assuming it is also by then a member). Portugal (and maybe Finland) might well join with Greece as a 'possible' rather than a 'probable'.

If the start is delayed until 1999 the situation will not be very different, indeed some countries could have taken a step backwards. If, however, the system is set up in 1997 with only those countries we describe as 'almost certain to participate' actually in it, then we would expect the rest to join within the following five years.

We would expect the move to a single currency to take place, for the countries which are members of the EMU, within a period of less than a year. Thus the target date for the ecu is still 1997.

1

The Road to Monetary Union

The Maastricht treaty on Economic and Monetary Union is the result of a long period of evolution. There has been very rapid progress on European integration since 1984, and the negotiations stimulated by the Delors Committee of 1989 have been complex. They have culminated in the intergovernmental conferences during 1991. However, the fundamental features of the agreement stem from ideals derived from the very earliest days of the conception of the Community after the war. To understand the Treaty, therefore, we have to go back to its postwar origins.

The postwar international economic order

The postwar economic order was dominated by the United States. The widespread destruction of the economic system in continental Europe led to heavy dependence on US funds for reconstruction. There was also widespread reliance on the US for the building up of a new security system, particularly as the polarisation between east and west became clear. The system developed readily as the US was prepared to play that role of leadership and to help generate the stability of the international financial system, with the Bretton Woods system of fixed but adjustable exchange rates.

The Organisation for European Economic Cooperation was set up in 1948 to help the recovery and, within its auspices, the European Payments Union followed in 1950, to try to alleviate the problems of the dollar shortage and, through the Bank for International Settlements, organise a system of international payments among the European countries. The use of funds for reconstruction on top of this produced a viable system even if it did not go as far as Keynes and some of its original architects envisaged, with the development of an international currency.

The Bretton Woods system was not very open at its inception. Because of the dominance of domestic over international transactions after the disruption of the war and the existence of substantial controls on trade and payments, countries could exercise a measure of independence in their monetary policies in a way not true today. They were often able to sterilise their domestic currencies from the impact of fluctuations in international payments. The common link in the system came through the US dollar, to which each currency was pegged within narrow bands. The dollar in turn had a fixed parity with gold. The controls on capital flows gave the countries the scope to manage their exchange rates, provided they kept sufficient reserves to withstand short-run shocks.

For over twenty years that system dominated international transactions in Europe. It proved to be remarkably stable. There was the major realignment associated with the UK's devaluation in 1949, and two French realignments in the 1950s, but in general countries adhered to their narrow bands of fluctuations around the agreed central rates. This adherence meant that some countries, notably the UK, encountered a series of balance of payments problems, whenever they attempted to expand too rapidly.

The system therefore came under pressure, on the one hand from countries seeking a more flexible route to adjustment to external shocks, and on the other from the pressures on the United States, particularly from the Vietnam war, which meant that it found it increasingly difficult to act as the anchor for the whole system. Weaker currencies like sterling were seeking some means of trying to avoid the need to make major step devaluations, with their inflationary and other destabilising effects, while the stronger currencies sought something better than dependence on the US dollar.

One facet of the evolution of European monetary union is thus the response to the breakdown of that system at the end of the 1960s. This strand of evolution was based very much on the international financial system and concerned with the development of a stable system of foreign exchange to replace the fixed peg on the US dollar. It was a reflection of the success of the recovery of the European economies, particularly that of West Germany, and the emergence of a viable counterweight to the US, which had previously dominated both trade and payments. In 1950 US GNP per head was nearly four times that of the future EEC(6), whereas by 1969 it was only twice as large. Meanwhile the EC's share of OECD exports reached 40 per cent by 1969, double that of the US, which declined to 20 per cent.

In a sense it was the very success of the system in assisting the post war recovery which imposed the strains on it. As countries recovered and grew they developed their international trade to enter wider markets and continue to expand. This involved a reduction in the barriers between them, both through a series of multilateral reductions in tariffs and easing of quantitative restrictions under the auspices of the GATT (General

Agreement on Tariffs and Trade) and through other bilateral or regional agreements, including EFTA, the EEC, Commonwealth Preference and the Benelux union. Reductions in the barriers to trade both reduced countries' abilities to control their international payments and exposed them more widely to shocks from outside. In general it was the smaller among the industrialised countries which experienced this most obviously. (Although it was developing countries which experienced the greatest fluctuations, through variations in commodity prices, exposing them rather more harshly as they also gained independence from the various European empires.)

Integration in Europe

A second theme leading towards monetary union was based more firmly on the development of Europe itself. As the West European countries emerged from the postwar chaos so the discussion of the future face of Europe also developed. Much of that discussion involved a tighter relationship between the countries in some sort of union. This was not just a matter of economic concern but of much wider political interests, leading to the formation of the European Coal and Steel Community in 1951 and the European Economic Community in 1958, between Belgium, France, Italy, Luxembourg, the Netherlands and West Germany. Attempts to form a political community among these six countries failed in 1952 and the European Defence Community foundered on French opposition in 1954.

Although questions of monetary union were on the ultimate agenda even from the beginning they were clearly not a matter for immediate decision and therefore did not attract more than vague consideration, the major aim in this regard being freedom of movement of capital. The emphasis was more on 'economic union' in the formation of the EEC, involving cooperation and coordination among member states. Discussion of international currency systems remained largely in the domain of academics and a few visionaries.

Although there are substantial arguments about the ordering or sequencing, to use a more fashionable word, of the steps in the process of voluntary economic integration among countries, monetary union did not come high on the list. Indeed the debate is still alive, as the Bundesbank has been arguing recently that EMU will not work properly without closer political union. However, it is also argued by others that monetary union may not merely be one of the appropriate early steps but can be a major unifying force, other aspects of economic, political and social integration coming later on. One of the reasons for making it such an early step is the ease of its achievement through the banking system and its importance in the control of the economy. It is no coincidence that monetary union came right at the beginning of German unification in 1989, a point we come back to in subsequent chapters. However, for monetary union to adopt a leading role in integration, suitable mechanisms must exist for the automatic transfer of funds from surplus to deficit regions, which requires an open internal economy and considerable fiscal as well as monetary integration. This did not characterise the European economy of the early 1950s.

The main distinguishing feature of European integration since the war has been its voluntary nature, with countries perceiving it to be in their political and economic interests to be more closely related rather than having that requirement thrust upon them. Such processes have tended to be rather more limited in the past except as a response to a common external threat and hence there has been no obvious blueprint to follow and no neat definitions and preconceptions of what various concepts like common markets, economic, monetary and political unions might actually involve. (See Pelkmans, 1984, and El Agraa, 1985, for a discussion of these definitions.)

The European Economic Community always had high ambitions and a widely made mistake in the early economic literature was to describe it simply as a customs union, differentiating it from EFTA (the European Free Trade Association) as an organisation dedicated to the removal of tariffs on mutual trade in manufactured goods, only by virtue of the fact that it had a common external tariff, rather than allowing each member state to maintain its own tariffs on imports from third countries (Aitken, 1973, for example). Even in purely economic terms it was always envisaged that a much wider range of barriers to trade would be eliminated to establish a Common Market in which goods and services could flow freely throughout the Community. What was not clear was how that might be achieved, given the differences in tax regimes, technical rules and standards, to say nothing of the indirect restraints on trade and measures of domestic policy that favoured national producers through subsidies and other preferential agreements.

No clear distinction was made between what Kay and Posner (1989) have described as the Bismarckian and Jeffersonian routes to integration. The Jeffersonian route, based largely on the interstate arrangements in the US, is essentially liberalising in character, permitting the free movement of items approved by the local rules in their place of production or destination, with a minimum of new universal rules to govern commerce. The Bismarckian route on the other hand aims to produce a common market by agreeing common rules, that apply in all member states. This latter approach involves far more positive steps to achieve integration and is essentially a process of harmonisation. Furthermore, unlike EFTA, the EC has, with the Court, the Commission, the Parliament and the European Investment Bank, had more than the minimum of central institutions to manage a trading system.

Although the early Community was dominated in budgetary terms by the Common Agricultural Policy, which still accounts for over half the

Community's spending, there were further Community competences in social policy, regional policy, industrial policy and competition policy among others aimed at completing some form of common market. These were seen as part of the progress to the 'ever closer union', whose form was not spelt out but would involve closer economic, political and monetary union as well as some element of redistribution to assist the development of the less advantaged parts of the Community. Right from the outset, the EEC established a Monetary Committee under Article 105 to 'review the monetary and financial situation in member states and the Community as a whole and to review the system of currency payments in the Community', opening the way to greater monetary cooperation and integration.

The nature of such a union among the member states was widely interpreted, from a United States of Europe, exhibiting a federal structure with states with rather greater powers than those in the United States of America, to a union of independent states, a Europe of Nations in the phraseology of de Gaulle, where the central institutions would have relatively limited powers and the existing nation states would remain as the principal entities. (It has been very obvious during the last couple of years that, although this debate has evolved considerably, the distinction of views still exists, with the UK holding a position more towards the Europe of Nations concept than do the other member states, for whom some sort of 'federal' structure could be acceptable.) In practice, even after the intergovernmental conference on 'political union', culminating in the Maastricht agreement, the nature of any longer-run political arrangement among the member states is far more tenuously described than that of economic and monetary union. Indeed it is the monetary union proposals which are the most highly developed. Here the institutions are set out, the form of timetable laid down and the competences established, as described in Chapter 2. Economic union on the other hand is still part of an evolving process, where legislative changes are being put in place but their consequences are far from clear (see, for example, Shipman and Mayes, 1990, and the wider ESRC research initiative, The Evolution of Rules for a Single European Market, NIESR, 1992).

The process of reducing tariffs and eliminating trade restrictions proceeded very much to timetable in the early years of the Community's existence, as it involved removing restrictions rather than coming to common agreements on new harmonised systems. Indeed the last tariffs were removed in 1968, some eighteen months ahead of schedule. (EFTA, which was formed later, in 1960, and set a faster timetable for tariff removal, also found that it could implement these changes more rapidly.) Progress in establishing the CAP was also steady, coming into force in 1962. The way forward in other areas proved rather more elusive as all the member states had to agree on the detail of harmonised systems. There were considerable disagreements of some issues and even a period when France did not participate fully, leaving 'an empty chair' at meetings.

This last controversy, ended by the 'Luxembourg compromise' of 1966, which established the rule of unanimity in the Council, was generated largely by the establishment of the concept of 'own resources', whereby the Community got its own funds to administer the CAP through the levies on imports from non-member states, a milestone in the process of fiscal integration.

The Commission put forward proposals in 1962 to move towards monetary union by 1971 in three stages; it is interesting to note that the idea of a three stage approach stretches back 30 years. Initially this was to involve greater consultation and cooperation over financial, economic and monetary policies among finance ministers and central bank governors. Although the proposals were not adopted, the Committee of Governors of Central Banks of the EEC was set up in 1964, along with a Budgetary Committee and a Medium-Term Economic Policy Committee.

As early as the late 1960s it was clear that further measures would have to be taken if progress towards closer union was to be advanced significantly. This, therefore, provided the second thread of an internal, European-derived, set of pressures towards closer economic and monetary union, which was occurring while the international framework was also under strain. Taken together this increased the chance that the European countries would produce 'European' solutions to the international difficulties. The balance of economic power in international trade and payments had moved strongly towards them in the previous two decades and they wished to advance joint action for its own sake. Had the EC moved forward earlier with its own ideas for European monetary cooperation and the Bretton Woods system survived longer we might have seen a very different path for European monetary history and quite possibly the international system as a whole.

The precursor to Maastricht in the 1970s

The main decisions of principle, to move towards economic and monetary union, were taken in 1969. The 'Barre Report' from the Commission set out the need for greater coordination of economic and monetary policies and the establishment of short-term and medium-term monetary support facilities. After discussions in Council, the summit of heads of state in The Hague at the end of the year called for the establishment of EMU, by three stages, based on the Barre proposals.

This pressure resulted in the Werner Report of 1970, which set out what the objectives of closer union were in much more exact terms as an economic and monetary union 'in which goods and services, people and capital will circulate freely and without competitive distortions, without thereby giving rise to structural or regional disequilibrium' (Pierre Werner was Prime Minister of Luxembourg). It would further imply 'the total and irreversible convertibility of currencies, the elimination of margins of fluctuation in exchange rates, the irrevocable fixing of parity rates'. While the Werner Committee was still meeting, the Governors of the EEC Central Banks agreed to set up a short-term monetary support mechanism and the system of own resources was extended to cover agricultural import levies and payments from VAT in the member states, up to 1 per cent of a standardised base. (The medium-term financial assistance facilities were not agreed until March of 1971.)

The immediate similarities between the Werner proposals and those which have been agreed at Maastricht are further emphasised when we recall that central controls would also be required: 'creation of liquidity ... and monetary and credit policy would be centralised; monetary policy in relation to the outside world will be within the jurisdiction of the Community; and policies as regards capital markets would have to be unified'.

The report was not clear whether there would be an actual single currency or merely a de facto one from the locked exchange rates. However, it did recommend that central banking be organised on a basis similar to that of the Federal Reserve System in the US. Fiscal policy coordination was required and a new economic policymaking body was to be set up which would be responsible to the European Parliament. The coordination was intended to increase progressively. In the first or second stages of the process a European Fund for Monetary Cooperation was to be set up, to be integrated in the final Stage 3 into the central banking system. A series of indicators was to be used of the effectiveness of the coordination of monetary and fiscal policies, particularly to highlight any potentially dangerous departures from what was expected.

Thus, with only small exceptions, the Werner proposals are very much the precursor of Maastricht. Since the differences are so small it is of paramount importance to explain why it is that the new attempt to attain economic and monetary union should succeed where the plans of 21 years ago failed.

The Bretton Woods system finally collapsed in early 1971 at the same time that the Werner proposals were being adopted. This involved the ending of fixed parities, the floating of the major currencies against the dollar and the ending of convertibility of the dollar for gold at a fixed rate. In December 1971, at what is known as the Smithsonian agreement, the ten largest trading countries agreed to try to hold their currencies around new parities but within wider 4 per cent bands.

The first step by the Community in response was to try to stabilise EC exchange rates rather more closely by having only 2 per cent bands with respect to each other within the wider bands with respect to the dollar. This arrangement was described as the 'snake' as the EC exchange rates would move together in a band relative to the dollar (within the 'tunnel' of the agreed dollar fluctuations - however it did not prove possible to constrain the dollar exchange rate as planned and by 1973 the currencies were effectively floating and the idea of the tunnel was abandoned).

The European Monetary Cooperation Fund was set up in 1973 and in 1974 requirements were agreed to set annual guidelines for policies in the member states, consistent with increasing convergence, and member states were to put in place means of altering spending, tax and debt arrangements to respond to these guidelines.

In practice these arrangements were overtaken almost immediately by the pressures of the first oil crisis and the differential impact and responses of member states to it. The Werner plan therefore really did not get as good an opportunity to succeed as it might. However, it is also argued by Baer and Padoa-Schioppa (1988) that the plan was weakly conceived in a number of respects, most of which have now been addressed in the Maastricht agreement. First of all there was no means of compelling member states to follow guidelines towards convergence. Secondly there was no clear allocation of responsibilities among the various institutions for setting and achieving the objectives of policy. There was also an exaggerated view of the ability of the member states to achieve the necessary convergence with the instruments available. Finally they argue that the process lacked dynamism to move through the stages to EMU.

However, what is far more important is the economic development of the last twenty years and the progress of other aspects of European integration over the same period. The Werner Report came at the end of a period of considerable economic success and dynamic stability. Had that stability and growth continued, then the chances of achieving monetary union would have been greatly enhanced because many of the conditions of convergence, which we discuss in the next chapter, already existed and the process of increasing coordination of policy would have had a much shorter road to travel. Exchange rates were already fixed within narrow bands, inflation rates were low, as were unemployment rates outside the South of Italy, debt ratios and public sector deficits were, in general, within the target ranges laid down at Maastricht.

However, as subsequent history has shown, this would have been an unstable equilibrium, which would probably have fallen apart had the shocks from the US or the oil crises hit after monetary union was in place. Furthermore, capital movements were heavily restricted and freeing them up might have released very considerable pressures, making the final transition to irrevocably locked exchange rates impossible. The Europe of 1970 was much less integrated than the Europe of 1992. Trade patterns were more diverse, non-tariff barriers to the free flow of goods, services and labour abounded and fiscal systems and policy responses varied widely. For a monetary union to succeed it requires not just a framework of rules for its administration but the existence of an economic area which responds to shocks in a sufficiently homogeneous manner that the inability to change relative prices in parts of the area through exchange rates is not seen to reduce the relative welfare of those regions significantly. In an integrated area such variations are automatically compensated to a large extent, through the tax and benefit system, through regional policy and through the ability of those worst affected to move to other regions where prospects are better. The EEC of 1970 was a long way from those ideals. In the remainder of this chapter we show the extent to which these deficiences have been corrected during the ensuing years, first by considering the development of the European Monetary System, second by exploring the process of European integration and finally by examining the changes in the economic environment.

The European Monetary System

As we noted in the last section, the blueprint for the current agreement on monetary union was drawn up twenty years ago. The progressive locking of exchange rates has also been evolving over the same period, first with the snake and second with the European Monetary System, which was put into effect in March 1979. The snake has largely been regarded as a failure, as only the Benelux countries were able remain in the system throughout with West Germany and, although France, Ireland, Italy, Norway, Sweden and the UK had all participated at some stage, only Denmark was also in the system when it ended (table 1). However, it played an important role in developing the processes of cooperation between the European central banks, which are essential in bringing together the currencies in an EMU and highlighted the sorts of problems that occur and have to be dealt with if the system is to survive. Without the experience of the snake, the EMS could readily have fallen apart. Indeed had the EMS been implemented in 1971 instead of 1979 it would probably not have achieved the credibility necessary for survival.

The European Monetary system was set up in 1979 following the decision of the July 1978 European Council in Bremen to set up 'a zone of monetary stability in Europe'. In many respects it was primarily a tightening up of the previous arrangements to prevent mutual exchange rates from fluctuating outside a 2 per cent band round their central parities and an integration of a European currency, the ecu, into the system. Previously, the European Unit of Account (EUA) had been introduced in 1975 as a basket of the member states currencies to provide a common central unit, which was used as the accounting unit for the Community institutions from 1978 onwards. (For details and a good assessment of the EMS see Gros and Thygesen, 1988.) However, the EMS was also seen as a clear step towards economic and monetary union through trying to achieve economic convergence as well as monetary control. (The experience of the 1970s led to a general change in approach to macroeconomic policy, with an emphasis on monetary control primarily aimed at the control of inflation and a rejection of traditional 'Keynesian' policies of fiscal expansion to counter high unemployment. Thus an emphasis on joint monetary action had become the prime tool with fiscal cooperation as its necessary adjunct.)

During over a decade of operation the EMS has evolved very considerably and still has further to go. Portugal and Greece are still not members of the exchange rate mechanism (ERM) and Spain and the UK joined only in 1989 and 1990 and operate within a wider 6 per cent band. In the early years there were frequent realignments (see Chapter 7, table 1) seven in the first four years up to March 1983. This period saw a progressive upward realignment of the D-Mark and the Dutch guilder relative to the other currencies, particularly the lira. Since then realignments have been much more infrequent and with the exception of the Italian realignment within its bands and its simultaneous move from a 6 per cent band to the 2 per cent band there has not been a realignment since the beginning of 1987. This therefore has seen a change from something akin to a continuation of the snake to an increasingly fixed exchange rate system.

The EMS system has not evolved quite as envisaged. The idea originally was that the currencies would fluctuate relatively freely inside the intervention limits but that when the limits were reached there would be general intervention by the central banks. In practice, action has been taken earlier and there has been intervention inside the margin, largely undertaken by the banks in the countries approaching the lower edge of the band. The system has become increasingly dominated by the role of the German Bundesbank, whose policy has determined the general strategy of economic policy in the other member states, hindering the ambitions of those for whom growth is more important.

The role of the ecu as a European currency has also evolved rather differently from that which was expected. The official ecu has had rather limited uses. It has been a currency of settlement but not generally one of intervention, as it could not be used for inframarginal intervention, prior to 1985, without a market. As the role of the dollar has declined, that of the D-Mark has increased, not that of the ecu. The private ecu has, on the other hand, blossomed. This ecu, composed of the member currencies in the same weights as the official ecu, has proved useful as a hedge against exchange risk and has offered a good rate of return compared with some other strong currencies. It is the second most important currency in net bond issuance but, despite growing encouragement from the Commission and member states, its growth is slowing, aided ironically by the growing convergence of the EC currencies and their rates of return, which means there is less need to use an intermediate composite currency. This private role was not fully thought out and as a result the system lacked some of the necessary payments systems which would have turned it into a more significant means of introducing a European currency. As it is, those people outside the banking sector receiving ecu instruments in

European transactions of relatively small size have often had difficulty converting them into domestic or other currencies.

Changes have been made in the borrowing facilities as the EMS has developed, extending the roles of both the medium-term financial support (MTFS) and very short term facility (VSTF). The major changes came after the experience in 1986-7, when external changes forced realignments rather than internal disequilibria. These changes are known as the Basle/Nyborg agreements (recommended by the central bank governors meeting in Basle and endorsed by the economics and finance ministers (ECOFIN) at their Nyborg meeting). In practice, these changes, which have recognised the need for intramarginal intervention, seem to have improved the ability of the system to survive external shocks, including almost immediately the October 1987 US stock market crash and its reverberation round the world and a bout of speculative pressure in September 1988. They tried to make the responsibility for intervention more symmetric so that all central banks have a responsibility for maintaining the integrity of the system, not just those whose currencies are under threat at the lower boundary of the range.

The EMS has thus developed into a very stable system for a number of reasons. Its practitioners have improved their techniques and changes in the rules of the system have made it easier to defend parities and to get cooperative action from all the participating central banks, not just from those whose currencies are at risk. At the same time there has been considerable convergence both in policy objectives and in economic performance among the member states which makes the task of defending the rates rather easier. Together these provide many of the ingredients for the possible success of moves towards closer EMU. However, the most important ingredient has been the extensive development of the process of European integration.

Closer European integration

The most obvious changes in the EC during the 1970s and early 1980s were the three expansions which increased the Community from six to twelve countries in three stages, the UK, Denmark and the Irish Republic joining at the beginning of 1973, Greece in 1981 and Portugal and Spain in 1986. These accessions have considerably complicated the path of integration, not least because it has been necessary to get the agreement of twelve parties rather than six. Spain, Portugal, Greece and Ireland had a standard of living considerably below that of the other member states, which extended the process of convergence (an issue we return to in detail in Chapter 5). This meant that the Community needed an expanded approach to regional policy, cemented by the implementation of the European Regional Development Fund (ERDF) in 1975. The accession of the UK added a large country, which had a rather different structure and behavioural approach, that has resulted in a number of problems, the most recent of which is manifested in unique requirements for the UK in the Maastricht agreement (as set out in Chapter 2).

Perhaps the most dramatic and certainly rapid expansion of the Community is the most recent one, involving the unification of East and West Germany and the incorporation of the whole in the Community, within a space of just a few months in 1990. The small size of the addition and the dominant role that West Germany is playing in assimilating the new area has meant that, despite extensive derogations, the impact on the rest of the Community has been limited. The change-round in Germany's budgetary and trade positions has placed a strain on interest rates throughout the Community, however, and the change in the pattern of German investment has raised worries in some of the less favoured regions in other member states that the path of their relative improvement will now be more difficult.

The developments in the whole of central and eastern Europe and the potential expansion of the EC within the foreseeable future to a Community of as many as 32 states transforms the prospects for the progress not just to economic, political and monetary union but to the whole scope and nature of the integration process. This is such a large question that we consider it separately in Chapter 6.

Progress on developing the integration of the Community, in terms of implementation of new measures, proved relatively slow in the years after 1968. The relative emphasis on harmonisation meant that agreement proved elusive in many areas and laborious in others. Indeed the major progress was made by Court judgements, particularly that on the Cassis de Dijon case in 1978, which established the principle of mutual recognition, emphasising that local rules could not be used to exclude products produced according to the rules of another member state. This opened the gates to a more comprehensive attack on the non-tariff barriers to trade.

By contrast with the years before, 1985 to date has seen a whirlwind of activity in Community decision-making. This process began with the the decision to tackle the whole network of measures imposed by member states, for a variety of domestic reasons, which in practice inhibit the operation of a single internal market in goods, services, capital and labour. These were set up in a White Paper, published in June 1985, containing nearly 300 areas in which action was required if the physical, fiscal and technical barriers to completing the internal market were to be removed. Furthermore it set a target date for completing the implementation of these measures at the end of 1992.

The White Paper did not increase the scope of the Communities' ambitions, it merely spelt out what was needed to achieve some of the intentions set out in the Treaty of Rome in 1956. Its contribution came in its comprehensiveness and the speed at which it hoped to achieve the change.

Agreement on the measures of economic integration is very much a political process but that process can lead or lag the aspirations of the market. By 1985 the process of legislative integration was lagging the practical integration of the market by firms. The process of internationalisation of production and distribution had become highly developed. European companies were losing market share in traditional areas to Japanese companies and, following a period of relative success in the US, after the consequences of the major budget deficit spilled over into a trade deficit, were losing out to the American response. Fragmentation of the European market, because different rules applied in the various member states for registering products and for the standards to which they had to comply, meant that European companies tended to face a 'home' market that was smaller and higher cost than those of their US and Japanese competitors. Practices of government procurement and industrial support also meant that existing divisions were emphasised rather than being eliminated. Barriers at the frontier slowed the transit of goods and restrictions on transport made deliveries more complex, between them making adoption of Japanese style just-in-time manufacturing methods and other aspects of flexible production more difficult to achieve.
    Industry was thus tending to lead the political decision makers and the European Round Table had earlier put forward a plan of its own to achieve a single market in five years (by 1990). There was, therefore, a momentum to achieve what might be described as microeconomic integration in Europe. The removal of tariff and quantitative barriers to trade was only a step in that process. Questions of macroeconomic coordination, monetary control and closer alignment of exchange rates may have helped create conditions which encouraged integration at the level of the firm and of the market players but they did not enable it. The 1992 programme is creating an integration of a far more detailed and pervasive nature, one which converts the interest in monetary union from a largely macroeconomic perspective to one of microeconomic benefit as well. The prospects for monetary union are thus very different for the period after 1992 than they were in 1970 at the time of the Werner Plan or in 1979 when the EMS was established.
    The White Paper measures were only part of the process of achieving this dramatic change in the process of integration. The Single European Act, which was signed in February 1986, coming into force in July 1987, not only embodied these aspirations into a new treaty but it established mechanisms which would help break the logjam that had held up the previous piecemeal attempts to advance the process of microeconomic integration. The move towards qualified majority decision-making in most areas related to the single market, rather than unanimity, has vastly increased the pace at which decisions can be taken. Although it may appear that unanimity is often still used in many cases, the practice is that those in the minority extract what concessions they can in the bargaining stage but

then agree to the final proposal when that process has been exhausted, or at any rate register only symbolic opposition.

The Single European Act goes far further than the narrow economic concerns, increasing the role of the European Parliament and setting objectives and requiring action in the fields of monetary policy, economic and social cohesion, social policy and research and technological development. The process did not stop there, as the Brussels Council in 1988 agreed a package of flanking measures, including further reform of the Common Agricultural Policy and a doubling of the structural funds to provide a substantial increase in the developmental assistance for the least favoured regions of the Community in Greece, Portugal, Ireland, parts of Spain and Southern Italy.

These measures are intended to increase the scope of convergence of the Community from integration of markets to a distribution of the gains throughout the regions. These aims are very clearly set out in Padoa-Schioppa's (1987) book on Efficiency, Stability and Equity. Macroeconomic concerns, particularly through the EMS and associated monetary measures, had focussed very much on trying to establish more stable conditions for growth. The single market measures, on the other hand, were aimed principally at increasing the efficiency of economic organisation within the Community. This left the dimension of equity which, as we suggest in Chapter 5, may be the key to the successful achievement of EMU throughout the Community. Equity is being addressed through the social dimension and through the use of the structural funds. However, budgetary equity, achieved for the UK in the 1980s by the Fontainbleau Agreement, is still to be negotiated and it is clear that many of the interests in the process of integration conflict.

While the structural funds try to ensure that the potential benefits of closer integration are achievable by all parts of the Community, the social dimension is intended to ensure that the benefits to industry are also spread to the personal sector both to people in the workplace and elsewhere - to the employed and the non-employed. To an extent this was embodied in the Social Charter (Community Charter of Basic Social Rights for Workers), published in 1987, and the Social Action programme of some 50 measures that were thought necessary to implement it. This social charter covers free movement of persons throughout the Community, fair treatment of the employed, vocational training, workplace consultation, health, safety and working conditions and the treatment of the disadvantaged.

Some of the motives for agreeing the social dimension have been rather mixed. Some of the countries with more extensive programmes of social provision have feared that there might be some form of 'social dumping', whereby those countries with lesser provision could undercut them by offering lower labour costs to mobile international producers and also that the more dependent sections of their communities would emigrate to take advantage of the better provision. These twin forces would add to unemployment in the areas of high social provision through successful competition for the location of productive activity and increase the burden on contributors for the support of immigrants. The UK has expressed continuing doubts on the need for some aspects of the social dimension and worries about their adverse effect on competitiveness. As a result the UK did not adopt the Social Charter and, as is explained in the next chapter, has not agreed to the inclusion of the 'social chapter' in the new treaty drawn up at Maastricht.

The intention and the result of these various programmes is not of course the same thing. Although the single market measures will go a long way to reducing barriers, they will go nowhere near creating single markets in the sense that they exist in the United States, Japan and Australia. Barriers of language, custom and local preferences will take generations to break down and many may never be eliminated (nor indeed is it necessarily in the economic, let alone social or political, interests of the Community to do so). Pressures for local autonomy and the importance of 'subsidiarity' (allocation of responsibility for executing EC policy to the member states, rather than Community institutions, where this is efficient and avoids substantial spillover effects) indicate that the underlying diversity of the Community is something that it will wish to retain. In practice there has been very little migration, although the member states are very sensitive to it, and the degree of relocation in the lower labour cost regions has been rather limited, with rationalisation tending to occur among the regions of industrial strength in the more central parts of the Community. Consequently, the less advantaged appear to be facing a more severe burden of adjustment.

The European market will continue to be driven by the forces of international competition rather than its own concerns, as the market is being opened up to establishment by firms from any country not just from the member states. The fears that the single market might create some form of 'Fortress Europe', whereby external barriers to trade were made more effective and a concerted programme of European industrial support was developed, as envisaged by some members of the Round Table of Industrialists, have largely been allayed (although the strong anti-dumping policy helps maintain some of the fears). Much of the significance of the single market comes from the fact that it extends international competition from the traditional area of manufactured goods to the whole of the private sector (and some public services). By freeing up the movement of capital all firms have the potential to benefit from this and invest where they think the conditions are best. The effects of this expansion of opportunity have been seen most obviously in the field of financial services as creating the free movement of capital, which as a necessary precursor for monetary union involves Community-wide access to international financial services.

Agriculture has not been an explicit part of the process of integration of the Community in recent years but, in practice, it is playing a crucial role. The success or failure of the Uruguay Round is going to have a major impact on the conduct of international trade policy over the coming years. At present the negotiating parties have managed to manipulate the discussions so that overall success appears to hinge on the making of further concessions on agriculture by the EC. The United States is seeing the upsurge of protectionist feeling that accompanies a presidential re-election period (Woolcock, 1990). A more acrimonious approach to commercial policy could easily destabilise the exchange rate system and set back the progress to EMU for reasons other than the success of the internal integration of the Community. Establishing a more equitable budgetary balance within the Community itself also involves a downgrading of agricultural price support relative to other programmes designed to improve cohesion in a period where budgetary expansion is unlikely to be popular.

In 1988 the pressure for continuing integration moved on with the directive requiring full liberalisation of capital movements by July, 1990, being agreed in June (with some derogations) and the 'Delors Committee' of central bank governors and two experts, chaired by the President of the Commission, to study and propose concrete steps to the achievement of EMU by stages, being set up in the same month by the Hannover Council. This and the subsequent progress to the intergovernmental conferences on economic, political and monetary union we consider explicitly in the next chapter.

The economic transformation of the Community

The European Community of 1968 showed very considerable 'convergence' in a number of macroeconomic respects, exchange rates, inflation, debt ratios, external and internal balance, as we noted above. In the intervening years that convergence and stability was severely disturbed, first by the collapse of the Bretton Woods system and the first two oil shocks and second by the expansion of the Community itself to include six new and rather diverse member states. Those two sources of destabilisation are now being overcome. We have already noted how exchange-rate stability has increased but this process of convergence has been much more widespread including not just nominal variables like price inflation and interest rates but real characteristics of the economy as well.

The creation of an integrated Community involves increasing 'convergence' of economic behaviour in a number of respects - policy, structure and behaviour. If the structure of the various member states is particularly different in terms of patterns of production, trade and structure of assets and liabilities, then their response to external shocks will tend to be different, particularly in terms of prices and employment. We have already cited the case of countries with oil and gas reserves, whose rates of exchange tended to rise as a result of the first and second oil crises, relative to those of their European partners, who did not have such resources. In the same way, a larger exposure to dollar imports has a greater impact on domestic prices from changes in the dollar exchange rate. In these circumstances the adjustment costs to a member state for an external shock may very well be less if it has a separate exchange rate. By varying prices it may be possible to ease the structural adjustment required and reduce the aggregate unemployment cost in the process.

The same inequity in the response may occur if the systems of economic policy are widely different, this may include the degree to which the system of taxes and benefits provides anticyclical support, through the release of investment reserve funds, for example. More important may be the differences in behavioural responses to the same shocks. Some member states are able to come to more consensual decisions about the levels of wage increases that can be afforded under conditions of inflationary pressure and hence adjust to the shock with lower unemployment costs. Each of these differences will both encourage and compel countries to break away from a permanent fixed exchange rate system to ease the costs of adjustment.

Over the 1970s and 1980s these sources of difference have been reduced by the process of integration. Trade patterns have been becoming increasingly dominated by mutual trade, reducing the importance of differences in exposure to foreign currencies. There has also been a measure of integration in the structure of production. However, the new members of the Community substantially reduced the degree of convergence in the short run. We have already noted a number of dissimilarities for the UK. Ireland, Spain, Portugal and Greece also showed clear structural differences, in particular from a greater emphasis on agriculture. The product composition of the latter three countries is of course different in character because of their Mediterranean location. Their policy and behavioural responses were also different. Social provision via the state tends to be lower.

The existence of these differences is a matter of fact but whether they are sustainable in an EMU is also a matter of political decision-making. The process of increasing integration of industry, rule systems, cooperation between governments and other authorities all tend to reduce these differences. In Chapter 4 we discuss whether these differences will be eliminated sufficiently in the run-up to EMU for it to be implemented in practice. Chapter 7 looks at the problems country by country.

However, the main focus of convergence in the popular literature and in the terms of the Maastricht agreement is on a set of nominal variables, including inflation, interest rates, internal and external balance, and public debt ratios. If countries have too high rates of inflation compared with the target level at the time of the final locking of exchange rates they will tend to find that the adjustment costs are politically unacceptable. These, however, are principally problems of the transition to EMU rather than of its sustainability or suitability. Similarly countries with high public and external debt ratios will tend to find that the service costs of these debts are difficult to sustain and that actions will need to be taken to reduce them. Here and in the case of the large budget deficit the concern is not just for the adjustment problems of these particular countries but for the burden that they will impose on the others if they fail to adjust.

One last aspect of convergence, or rather the lack of it, has also characterised the 1970s and 1980s. As is shown in chart 1, Spain, Portugal, Greece and Ireland had been steadily closing the gap between their real GDP per head and that of the rest of the Community in the 1960s. Indeed had that rate of convergence continued Spain would by now have closed the gap completely. Since the first oil crisis, however, that process of clear convergence has been absent. In recent years, assisted by the transfers within the EC, Ireland, Spain and Portugal have begun to narrow the gap again, however the gap for Greece has actually widened.

There is no reason why an integrated Community should not operate with the prevailing range of diversities in real incomes and other indicators of the real standard of living. However, integration in itself tends to imply the wish to reduce the extent of such differentials. In the context of the EC, the question at issue is whether the costs of transition for the less advantaged countries will be sufficiently offset by the increased real convergence offered by membership of the Communities. We consider this question in Chapter 5. At this stage, we can merely note, from the experience of the last twenty years, that there is no obvious conclusion that the unaided process of development will lead to a narrowing or widening of differentials. Hence the less advantaged may very well feel that they wish to see more coming from the process of integration than maintenance of the relative status quo.

The basis for Maastricht

In the case of the 'completion of the internal market' and the proposals for economic and monetary union, the political decisions to try to proceed were taken before the economic justifications were presented. Monetary union has been presented as a necessary adjunct to a properly operating single market and it is clear that it offers major microeconomic benefits in its own right, in reducing transactions costs and removing exchange-rate uncertainty between the member states, which should result in clear welfare and growth gains. There will be further macroeconomic improvements from the joint attempt to achieve the aim of monetary stability, particularly for those member states which are particularly inflation prone at present.

What the pattern of European integration since the war has shown is that monetary union has been assigned a high priority within the EC right from the early days. However, it has only been with the continuing integration of the European economies, particularly the progress to the single market and the experience with managing an orderly exchange rate system, that proceeding to EMU has become really feasible rather than a desirable sounding long-run aim. The evolution of that integration over the next few years will show whether that aim is really attainable.

The oil shocks and the long learning process to develop a new order to replace the Bretton Woods system have delayed progress towards monetary union in Europe and revealed not just its difficulty but the ability to overcome those difficulties. EMU offers two major facets in this context, the largely microeconomic extention of benefits from a further step in the process of ever closer union in Europe and the benefit to the macroeconomic policy aim of monetary stability, through the particular structure of the system that has been proposed at Maastricht. This puts the control of inflation as the main aim and is intended to provide the independence to the central banking system necessary to achieve it through the operation of monetary policy and the cooperation of the member state governments in the approriate operation of fiscal policy.

These are considerable ambitions and we consider in the next chapter how the Maastricht agreement plans they should be achieved and the way the argument developed, that resulted in them, following the decision of the Hannover Council in 1988 to set up the Delors Committee.

Table 1 *History of the Snake*

Date		Change
1972	April	Snake established
	June	£ floated, sterling leaves the snake
	Dec.	Lira leaves
1973	March	Joint float agreed, D-Mark revalued by 3%
	June	D-Mark revalued by 5½%
	Sept.	Guilder revalued by 5%
	Nov.	Norwegian kroner revalued by 5%
1974	Jan.	French franc leaves
1975	July	French franc rejoins
1976	March	French franc leaves;'worm' agreement for narrower bands between Benelux currencies abandoned.
	Oct.	Realignment, D-mark up by 6% against Danish krone, 3% against Swedish krona and Norwegian krone and 2% against Benelux
1977	April	Swedish krona devalued by 6%, Danish and Norwegian kroner by 3%
	August	Swedish krona leaves
		Norwegian and Danish kroner devalued by 5%
1978	Feb.	Norwegian krone devalued by 8%
	Oct.	Realignment, mark up 4% against Danish and Norwegian kroner and by 2% against Benelux
1979	March	EMS comes into effect

Source: *Brooks (1979)*.

Chart 1 *The evolution of disparities among the member states*

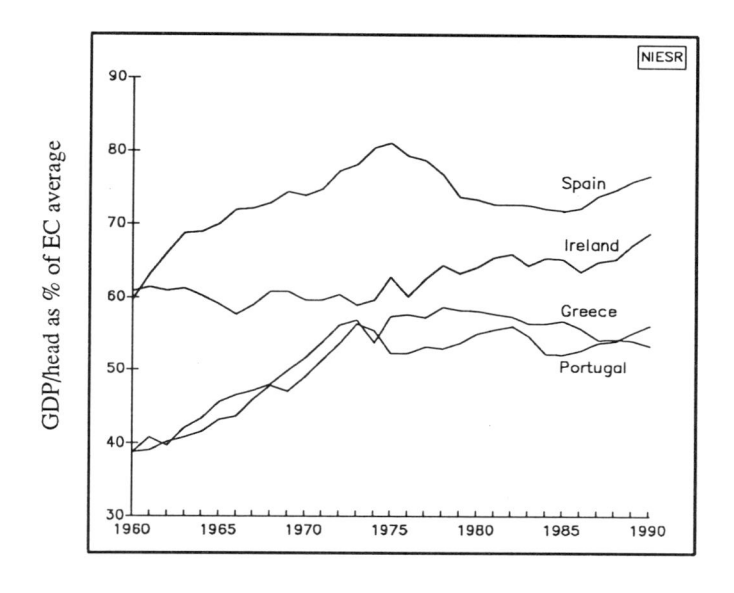

2

The Maastricht Treaty on EMU

The general form of the Maastricht Treaty evolved steadily from its antecedents, stretching back at least as far as the Werner Plan of 1970, through the discussions of the Delors Committee of 1988–9 to the intergovernmental conferences of 1990–1. Nevertheless there were some surprises, for outside observers at least, in the final conclusions which were agreed at the European Council at Maastricht in December, 1991, for ratification by the member states during 1992. This chapter explores the nature of the agreement and arguments used for rejecting some of the other options available.

The main provisions

The Maastricht agreement produced a new treaty on European Union to replace the existing Community treaties, as amended by the Single European Act of 1986. Thus while the Treaty of Rome was able to cover the main issues for 30 years, the pace of integration has proved so great recently that the treaties have required amendment twice in six years. Originally, when the Hannover Council set up the Delors Committee in June 1988, it was expected that the new treaty would cover the necessary extra provisions to set up economic and monetary union. When the Madrid Council, a year later, decided to implement the first stage of the Delors Committee proposals on 1 July 1990 and to set up an intergovernmental conference to sort out the measures necessary for the subsequent stages, it was only EMU that they refered to. However, largely as the result of a Franco-German initiative, the special Dublin Council of April, 1990, confirmed its commitment to 'political union' and set up a parallel intergovernmental conference on the treaty provisions necessary to strengthen the democratic legitimacy of the union. It also set a deadline for both intergovernmental conferences to complete their proposals in time for ratification by the member states before the end of 1992.

The result is a *Treaty on European Union,* signed on 7 February, 1992, whose provisions are set out in table 1. It emphasises not just convergence to achieve EMU but cohesion and progress on other fronts and a determination to continue the process of creating an ever closer union among the peoples of Europe. EMU is a stage in the process, not the end of it, not just because of the potential for widening the Community but because of the intention of deepening it further.

Table 1 *The preamble to the Maastricht Treaty on European Union*

The signatories to the Treaty

RESOLVED to mark a new stage in the process of European integration undertaken with the establishment of the European Communities

RECALLING the historic importance of the ending of the division of the European continent and the need to create firm bases for the construction of the future Europe

CONFIRMING their attachment to the principles of liberty, democracy and respect for human rights and fundamental freedoms and the rule of law

DESIRING to deepen the solidarity between their peoples while respecting their history, their culture and their traditions

DESIRING to enhance further the democratic and efficient functioning of the institutions so as to enable them better to carry out, within a single institutional framework, the tasks entrusted to them

RESOLVED to achieve the strengthening and the convergence of their economies and to establish an economic and monetary union including, in accordance with the provisions of this Treaty, a single and stable currency

DETERMINED to promote economic and social progress for their peoples within the context of the accomplishment of the internal market and of reinforced cohesion and environmental protection, and to implement policies ensuring that advances in economic integration are accompanied by parallel progress in other fields

RESOLVED to establish a citizenship common to the nationals of their countries

RESOLVED to implement a common foreign and security policy including the eventual framing of a common defence policy which might in time lead to a common defence thereby reinforcing the European identity and its independence in order to promote peace, security and progress in Europe and in the world

REAFFIRMING their objective to facilitate the free movement of persons, while ensuring the safety and security of their peoples, by including provisions on justice and home affairs in this Treaty

RESOLVED to continue the process of creating an ever closer union among the peoples of Europe in which decisions are taken as closely as possible to the citizen in accordance with the principle of subsidiarity

IN VIEW of further steps to be taken in order to advance European integration

HAVE DECIDED to establish a European Union

24 Achieving Monetary Union in Europe

Since the treaty is divided into 'titles' and 'chapters' it is possible to sort out the elements which refer to economic and monetary union easily. However, the drafters have taken the opportunity to amend a wide range of clauses in the existing treaty and an exposition of them would take a book in itself. Several of these also impinge on EMU. The principal proposals in the economic and monetary union section are as follows: the new treaty sets out the nature, functions and constitution of the new central banking system which is to manage the single currency, monetary policy and foreign exchange in the new monetary union. It also explains how fiscal and budgetary policy are to be managed. However, our primary interest focuses on the proposals for organising the transition to monetary union.

Monetary union, as in the Werner and Delors proposals, is intended to take place in three stages. The first stage has already commenced with the freeing of capital flows and the integration of financial markets under the single market programme. That programme in itself provides a major plank in the establishment of what is described as 'economic union'. Stage 2 involves the creation of a new Community institution, the European Monetary Institute (EMI). The EMI is purely a transitional institution which will cease once it has been successful in bringing the Community to the start of Stage 3 and be replaced by the European Central Bank (ECB). The ECB together with the central banks of the member states form the European System of Central Banks (ESCB) from the beginning of Stage 3.

The role of the EMI is to oversee the transition when Stage 2 begins on 1 January, 1994. It has roles of planning, monitoring and advising. In the transition, the member states' institutions have responsibility for the execution of monetary, exchange rate and fiscal policy and the EMI is intended to help with the process of increasing coordination among them. However, it is not until Stage 3 that the ECB takes over responsibility for exchange rate and monetary policy. How exactly the ECB will function is to be established during the transition. What has been set out in the treaty is its objectives, constitution and the nature and composition of the board which will run it. Indeed in this transition period all the institutions involved, the national central banks and the governmental and other bodies involved in fiscal, financial and monetary operation and regulation will have to undergo a learning process in cooperation to prepare for Stage 3. National legislation for their own central banks will have to be compatible with the statute of the ESCB, for example.

However, the most important feature of the transition from the point of view of the present discussion is that for member states to participate in the monetary union they have to meet four criteria of convergence:

1 **a high degree of price stability** '... apparent from a rate of inflation which is close to that of at most the three best performing Member States in terms of price stability'. In the associated protocol this is defined as 'price performance that is *sustainable* and an *average rate of inflation, observed over a period of one year* before the examination, that does not exceed by more than 1 percentage points that of at most the three best

performing Member States in terms of price stability ' (inflation to be measured by comparable Consumer Price Indices).

2 **a sustainable government financial position**, 'apparent from having achieved a government budgetary position without a deficit that is excessive'. The associated protocol defines this position in two respects: a maximum 3 per cent for the ratio of the planned or actual government deficit to GDP at market prices; a maximum 60 per cent for the ratio of government debt to GDP at market prices. (In this context the government is defined as general government, excluding commercial operations, the deficit is net borrowing and debt, total gross debt consolidated across the government sector.) The governments of the member states have an obligation under this protocol to ensure that their policies achieve these targets.

3 **observance of the normal fluctuation margins provided for by the ERM of the EMS** for at least two years, without devaluing against any other member state currency.

4 **the reflection of the durability of convergence in long-term interest rate levels.** The associated protocol defines this as a divergence not exceeding 2 percentage points from the nominal long-term government bond rates of at most the three best performing member states in terms of price stability.

However, in determining the readiness for stage 3 the Commission and the EMI also have to take account of: *the development of the ecu, the results of the integration of markets, the situation and development of the balances of payments on current account, and the development of unit labour costs and other price indices.*

The actual decision over whether to go ahead is a complex process.

First of all the Council acting by qualified majority has to decide on the basis of the various recommendations we have just described:

1 whether each individual member state fufils the necessary conditions for the adoption of a single currency.

2 whether a majority of the member states fulfils the necessary conditions for the adoption of a single currency

and then, in turn, recommend its findings to the Council, meeting in the composition of heads of state/government (which will also have the benefit of an opinion from the European Parliament). If that meeting agrees that a majority of the member states meets the conditions *then* it must decide, *acting by qualified majority*, whether it is appropriate for the Community to enter stage 3 and if so to set a date [emphasis added].

This meeting must take place before the end of December 1996.

If by the end of 1997 the date for starting stage 3 has not been set then stage 3 will start on 1 January, 1999. The Council must meet in the composition of heads of state/government before 1 July, 1998 to decide which member states fulfil the conditions of convergence for participation. (The question of a majority is no longer relevant.)

Stage 3

It is in Stage 3 that the full EMU begins to operate managed through the new institutional arrangements of the ECSB, the ECB and the Economic and Financial Committee. This will generate all the requirements for the operation of a single monetary policy, foreign exchange policy and the coordination of economic policy. However, the treaty makes it clear that while the implementation of the ecu as the single currency of Europe is the objective, this will follow the irrevocable fixing of exchange rates at the start of Stage 3 and not occur right at the outset:

> 'these activities shall include the irrevocable fixing of exchange rates leading to the introduction of a single currency, the ecu' [Article 3a].

Although it is stated that there should be a timetable for this transition, the treaty does not say when the single currency should be introduced during Stage 3. The bulk of the sections on Stage 3 focus on the constitution and operation of the new central bank.

The form of the ECSB and the constitution of the ECB

It is the ECSB, composed of the national central banks and the ECB, which has the objective of maintaining price stability. Without prejudice to that objective it has to support the Community's general economic objectives within a clear framework of free market principles. The ESCB has four tasks:- to define and implement monetary policy; to conduct foreign exchange policy; to manage the member states' foreign exchange reserves and promote smooth payments systems.

The ECB is the executive organisation in the system. It and all the national central banks are given independence from the institutions of the Community and member state governments in the exercise of their functions. The bank is run directly by a six-man Executive Board of a president, vice-president and four other members, who are appointed by the Heads of state/government after consulting the European Parliament and the Governing Council of the ECB, the period of office being a single term of eight years. That Governing Council is composed of the executive board and the governors of the national central banks. Voting is on a one man one vote basis, acting on a simple majority except where it refers to the bank's capital when votes are proportionate to the member states' subscribed capital, the executive board having no votes. The subscribed capital is determined by an equal weighting of the member states' shares of Community population and GDP at market prices (the latter averaged over the previous five years). The subscription is revised every five years.

The ECB is responsible for the note issue, open market operations, setting of minimum reserve requirements and other aspects of monetary control although they may be exercised through the national central banks. However, while the ECB can advise on prudential supervision of credit institutions and stability of the financial system, these functions remain the responsibility of the member states. The bank is subject to audit and is under the jurisdiction of the Court of Justice. Overdraft or other credit facilities by the ECB or national central banks to any Community or member state public body are explicitly prohibited.

The President of the Council and a member of the Commission may attend the Governing Council of the ECB. The ECB has to make an annual report on its activities which the President will present to the Council and the European Parliament. He and the other members of the Executive Board may be heard by the relevant committees of the parliament at either side's request.

The transition organisation, the EMI, has a Council composed of a President and the Governors of the national central banks and has the same guarantee of independence. While the primary tasks are to sort out the operating rules and procedures for the ESCB, the ECB and national central banks within it and advising the member states on the conduct of monetary policy, it also has an important role in the operation of the EMS, administering the VSTF and medium term financial assistance and the issuance of ecus to EC and third country institutions. The President is the executive officer; in his absence the Vice president, who is a governor of one of the national central banks, deputises. The EMI is subject to the same auditing and Court of justice jurisdiction as the ECB and, on the day stage 3 starts, transfers its assets and liabilities to the ECB, which will then liquidate it.

Economic policy

Matching these arrangements for monetary management is the chapter on economic policy. The principle is that member states shall regard their economic policies as a matter of common concern and coordinate them within the Council. The Council, acting on a recommendation from the Commission, will set out broad guidelines for the economic policies of the member states and the Community. There will be multilateral surveillance of economic developments and the consistency of policies with the guidelines. Should a member state's policy be judged inconsistent by a qualified majority on the Council, the Council can make recommendations to the member state, which it may choose to make public. In particular, the Commision will monitor the member states' budgetary and debt positions on the basis of the planned or actual ratios of the deficit to GDP and debt to GDP using the same criteria as set out in the convergence criteria for entry into stage 3. If the deficit is thought excessive after taking into account 'relevant factors', including whether it exceeds government investment then the Council can recommend action by the member state to remedy it. If the member state does not respond adequately to the recommendations then the Council can impose four sanctions: the requirement to publish further information before issuing bonds or securities; inviting the EIB to review its lending to the member state; requiring the member state to make a non-interest bearing deposit while the deficit remains excessive; levying a fine. In order to take these sanctions and even make the recommendations for action the Council has to act on two thirds majority of the votes cast — excluding the member state concerned — using the usual weighting system.

Other aspects of the Maastricht treaty directly impinging on monetary union
The new treaty addresses the question of social and economic cohesion in the Community and sets it a high priority (articles 130A and 130B). A new cohesion fund is also established and a Committee of the Regions composed of representatives from the regions of the member states to act in an advisory capacity in the same way as the Economic and Social Committee. Explicit protocols set out these intentions.

The nature of the new treaty and the compromises it involves

The Delors Committee report is very helpful in explaining what an economic and monetary union consists of and hence what needs to be implemented to achieve it. 'EMU in Europe would imply complete freedom of movement of persons, goods, services and capital, as well as irrevocably fixed exchange rates between national currencies and finally a single currency. This in turn, would imply a common monetary policy and require a high degree of compatibility of economic policies and consistency in a number of other policy areas, particularly in the fiscal field.' The monetary union requirements are rather more straightforward than those for economic union, which it suggests are (1) the single market (2) competition policy and other measures aimed at strengthening market mechanisms (3) common policies aimed at structural change and regional development, and (4) macroeconomic policies including binding rules for budgetary policies.

This is *a* definition rather than *the* definition of an economic union as the role and nature of competition policy; the extent of the 'single market' and the need for structural and regional policies are a choice rather than a requirement for all economic unions as the existence of unions which involve them in varying degrees shows.

There is an implied tendency, which perhaps reflects the composition of the Delors Committee, to suggest that specifying the rule system for EMU will ensure that it will work. In part, however, it reflects the wisdom in the Maastricht agreement of having a relatively slow timetable. The agreement lays down a set of general rules as to how the new system should operate. It is not a manual which, if read carefully by any intelligent and well intentioned government or central bank, would ensure the successful implementation and development of an EMU. It merely provides the framework in which such a system can evolve. Inevitably, as a framework for covering largely uncharted territory, unexpected difficulties will be encountered and detailed modifications will have to be made in operating practices. In the chapters that follow we trace out what will have to happen in practice if EMU is to function well, in particular how monetary policy may operate, how the regions of the Community will need to be able to adjust in the absence of the exchange-rate flexibility, how EMU can accommodate new members, while the second half of the book deals with the practicalities of handling the transitional arrangements set out in the Maastricht agreement. This chapter restricts itself to the agreement itself and the implications from the process of agreeing it.

The need to compromise
The Community has been rather good at meeting deadlines in recent years, as the progress on agreeing the 279 measures to implement the 1992 programme witnesses, and the completion of the agreement on schedule at the Maastricht Council was no exception. However, the eagerness to meet the timetable and the short notice for the proposals on political union have meant that there are rather more loose ends and untidy features to the agreement than might have been expected. The most obvious of these relates to what is referred to as the 'social chapter' of the treaty, which the UK refused to agree to and hence has been adopted as a separate protocol by the other eleven members. Derogations have been common in the past to permit specific member states to delay implementation of Community rules which gave them particularly difficult problems, such as the final abolition of capital controls by Greece, Ireland, Portugal and Spain. However, this appears to be the first time that a country has been able to opt out of an area of legislation entirely.

The monetary union component of the new treaty has not been immune from such compromises as the UK is given the right to come to an explicit decision whether to participate in the final stage of monetary union, once the Community as a whole has decided to go ahead with it. The Irish Republic and Denmark also have to have referenda before they can agree to entering stage 3. An unfortunate degree of uncertainty has thus entered the process, to say nothing of the uncertainty over timing and likely participants at the outset of stage 3 which are written into the treaty proposals. This is particularly unfortunate as one of the major requirements for EMU to work satisfactorily is credibility. Not only do the changes proposed have to be feasible but for businesses to adapt their behaviour towards its achievement and for the market makers in exchange and money markets to adjust their view of the prospects for inflation and the rate of return in the various member states, they must believe that EMU will occur within a finite timetable and that the specific countries will be full and irrevocable participants in it. Introducing uncertainty into who will be the eventual participants and into the timetable of implementation reduces the credibility of the process substantially. Having some flexibility in the transition procedure to ensure that EMU is not introduced prematurely and that the transition problems for those member states with the greatest difficulty are properly handled collaboratively by the Community is eminently sensible, but this is not how the draft treaty reads — it reflects disagreement among the negotiating parties.

The existence of disagreement is not a surprise, indeed it is the ability to come to an agreement given the scale of the change intended, the differences in initial opinions and the costs involved, which is so impressive. Furthermore, having come to a compromise, which was found satisfactory, the member states have the incentive to make the agreement work. The apparent uncertainty over the timing and membership of Stage 3 can be reduced rapidly by the actions of the member states and the Community in striving to achieve convergence over the next two or three years. It is, however, important to emphasise the areas where disagreement did occur in the negotiations as these are clearly the areas of greatest sensitivity, which have to be worked on carefully during the transition if the process is to be successful.

There are at least four main areas over which there was considerable disagreement of view over the form of the treaty as far as EMU was concerned: the aims and accountability of the ECB; the process of transition; the extent of economic union required especially in the social dimension; and the need for cohesion in the EC.

The aims and accountability of the ECB

The basic problem which had to be resolved over what the ECB should do and how it should be controlled is that there are several aims of economic policy. An example of the problem is set out at the beginning of the Delors Report (para 16) '*Economic and monetary union in Europe* ... would imply a common monetary policy and require a high degree of compatibility of economic policies and consistency in a number of other policy areas. These policies should be geared to price stability, balanced growth, converging standards of living, high employment and external equilibrium.' These policies inevitably conflict and within member states a compromise is reached as to which should be subordinated at any one time. However, the Bundesbank was very clear that a major contribution to the success of the German economy was the independence of the central bank and its unequivocal focus on the control of inflation.

Governments in other countries, like France, had the view that while controlling inflation was all important there were occasions when other objectives should come first, particularly in the short run. Most member states operated with the central bank ultimately subordinated to the wishes of the government, so while the bank might control the instruments of monetary policy and look after the immediate details it was the government, usually through the ministry of finance, which set the objectives of that policy and decided the fiscal and monetary stances. To some extent

The Maastricht Treaty on EMU 31

this was an argument over ideals, as although the governors of the Federal Reserve System operate with considerable independence and the Bundesbank operates in a legal framework of independence, the practice is that a degree of compromise is reached. In the US case this compromise is the result of 80 years evolution. The Federal Reserve Board does not overstep the mark and prejudice the integrity of government policy, although it could do so, while the executive and indeed the Congress do not exercise their full powers of intervention. The compromise works through there being clear and understood objectives for the Fed and a system of accountability, both when the Chairman is appointed and in the reporting and justifying of the Fed's activities to Congress. This particular balance between the executive, legislative and judicial arms of government is unique to the American constitution and any balance in the European EMU has to be both more complex because of the role of the individual member states and clearly spelt out because it is new and at the beginning of the learning process of how to make it work.

If a European Parliament or European Council got to the stage of wishing to remove a President of the ECB then the process of compromise would have failed. Like so many sanctions it is intended to work through the threat from its existence not through its execution. We have already seen in the German case that there are limits to the independence of the Bundesbank, whatever the constitution might say. The political imperatives of German unification were such that the government felt it had to take decisions on economic and monetary union, such as the one to one parity of the West and East German currencies, which might have undesirable inflationary consequences, because the alternatives might compromise the success of the exercise as a whole. Thus although the Bundesbank might protest and its President, Karl Otto Pöhl, resign — despite being a figure of international standing, tipped by many as the first President of the ECB — the government's view prevailed.

The balance wanted by many countries was that the Council of Ministers' view should ultimately prevail. From the German position the new single currency had to be at least as strong as the D-Mark if it was to be worth having and that this required a strong constitutional position for the ECB. Eventually this latter view was accepted but there was considerable argument about the balance of power even within the ECB's structure. Each country needed to be represented on the board of governors but the same compromise which faces all EC representation had to be addressed, should representation be equal for member states, related to population or to economic size? What sort of majority should be sufficient for action? Elaborate schemes were suggested but ultimately it became clear that if such a bank were to function effectively the executive committee must be able to act with considerable authority.

The resulting compromise is therefore towards the extreme of an independent policy, narrowly focussed on price stability, with a minimum of external controls, whether from the Council or from the European Parliament. It remains to be seen whether the role of the Parliament in the appointment of the President of the ECB and the periodic reports and examinations actually prove to be acceptable mechanisms of control and accountability. Whether the balance of the system as a whole functions satisfactorily can only be tested in practice when the first major price shocks rock the system. It is improbable that the Council in the form of the heads of state/government will not come to short-run decisions about how to act, which the ECB will have to adapt to. Nevertheless, the signatories have taken the sensible course of agreeing a clear definition of powers and hence have defined a clearcut, workable system based on existing central bank experience.

One example from outside the Community both illustrates the workability of the solution arrived at in Maastricht and the implicit tensions that can arise. The New Zealand government gave independence to its central bank, charging it with bringing down inflation to 0-2 per cent within five years. The most recent inflation figures show a slight fall in prices, largely as a result of the success in the bank's management and a relatively consistent government deficit policy. But the New Zealand economy has not prospered during that transition and the government is now faced by a low rating in the polls and very considerable public pressure to ease its fiscal stance (much of the current unpopularity stems not so much from the stance itself but from the social expenditure cuts and healthcare charges used to achieve it). As the next election looms the tension will be obvious. In New Zealand the government has to stand on its own. In EMU a problem of this nature, restricted to only some countries, can be eased by Community action. Short-term deficits can not only be condoned, without unleashing Community wide inflation, but medium-term finance is available to let a member state ride out the period of difficulty.

The process of transition
The negotiations over the process of transition were clouded by the conflict between the wish of member states not to be excluded from the benefits of EMU at the outset and the need to ensure that the terms of the EMU did actually confer the benefits, particularly in the form of control of price stability. The approach of the Delors Committee and the Commission throughout was that the Community should pass from one stage of EMU to the next when it was fit to do so. Thus stage 1 is entered when freedom of capital movements exists, stage 2 is begun when the coordination mechanisms are in place but stage 3 is not commenced until the member states have 'converged' in some sense. The alternative position put forward was that each stage imposes more effective sanctions on the member states because inflationary and depreciation routes to change are no longer available and that a cooperative solution to individual problems becomes easier as all have a vested interest in the successful adjustment of the states

with the greatest problems. This offers the potential threat that the difficulties of the weak could prejudice the whole system. In the agreed solution those with difficulties are excluded and the onus for putting them right is very much their own. In particular, it became rapidly clear that the convergence conditions thought necessary to ensure that the new system would be stable and non-inflationary were such that many countries would bear heavy costs in trying to achieve them and that the likelihood of all twelve achieving them in the reasonably close future was remote. It was argued by some therefore (Spain, for example), that membership of the EMU would help impose convergence and that budgetary compensation methods to less advantaged countries with budgetary problems in the transition would enable them to join from the outset. This would obviously imply a limited amount of extra inflation to the system as a whole in the short run but if the deficits were small by reference to Community rather than the member state's GDP then the result would be manageable. If the criterion were absolute, either EMU would be put off indefinitely as convergence would be likely to elude some or other state at any particular time or some would have to be left out. Once outside the system and having been shown to have failed to be able to achieve convergence, the fear was that credibility would be low and the costs of converging even higher so that participation could be put off for a long period.

The convoluted compromise over dates for starting stage 3 is an attempt to get round this. In the first instance the attempt can be made to try to get as many states as possible within the system. It is certain from the terms of the agreement that the minimum number of participants must be at least a simple majority (seven) but since the decision has to be by qualified majority in the Council a considerably higher number is likely, *if* the go ahead is to be given by the deadline of the end of 1996. After that date EMU will go ahead in 1999 (at the latest) with however many member states are deemed to have converged. As far as we can see from the technical conditions that union could consist of only one member state. That, of course, would be clearly ridiculous and render the concepts redundant but EMU for even quite a small core of five or six member states, such as with the initial Schengen agreement, could be a believable building block on the road to full EMU if other member states were clearly close to achieving convergence.

In effect the main argument has been postponed. If a significant number of countries do not meet the criteria at the first decision date it is unlikely that some of those still experiencing problems will be willing to see the others go ahead with an arrangement which would be to their competitive disadvantage (assuming that is that the list of benefits set out in *One market, one money* and elsewhere is believed to be correct). Whether they would still be willing to see such a step even in 1998/9 is also debatable. Such a multispeed Europe might be thought undesirable, hence the scope exists for a compromise on the convergence conditions to be applied. In any case we are unlikely to be discussing a Community of twelve in 1999 or indeed in 1997. The likely early members, Sweden, Austria and Finland, are better able to achieve convergence than most member states and hence will increase the chance of both a simple majority of states qualifying and of obtainining a qualified majority in the Council for going ahead at an early stage.

A second and fundamentally different proposal for the process of transition was made by the UK. Instead of this rule-based system and institutional approach to integration, the UK Treasury argued that an evolutionary approach would be more sensible, letting the ecu emerge as the single currency of Europe progressively. For this purpose they suggested creating a new 'hard' ecu, which would never be devalued relative to any member currency. Hence on any realignment the ecu would stay with the strongest currency. At the same time mechanisms would be improved for the use of the ecu and a European Monetary Fund would be set up to manage the system in the transition. If the ecu as a single currency really was the right way forward then market agents in both public and private sectors would adopt it progressively.

Part of the attractiveness of this proposition was that the opportunity for the wider use of the ecu and hence transactions costs savings for some firms could occur earlier in the transition as could more of the characteristics of an EMU. The obvious disadvantages were that introducing a further currency and running a common currency in parallel with the existing currencies (and indeed the existing ecus) would complicate the system in the short run. This might add to costs in net terms rather than reduce them and it would require a new institution and untried procedures to regulate it. In particular it would not be the responsibility of any particular central bank to manage it, hence it might result in the sorts of inflationary bursts that have accompanied other examples of financial deregulation. This latter problem could no doubt have been overcome but the overriding objection was that this proposal did not acknowledge that monetary union would necessarily be the outcome. It therefore received relatively little support from other member states and was viewed largely as a blocking or spoiling tactic rather than as a constructive proposal for trying to achieve more effective monetary integration.

As we pointed out in *A Strategy for the ECU* there is a lot to be said for the increasing use of the ecu in the transition. The existing proposals are very much aimed at the process from the point of view of the central banks and the management of the system, rather than at trying to maximise the benefits to the users and trying to confer as many of the advantages as possible from EMU to European customers and firms in the transition. This is perhaps to be expected from a set of proposals derived originally by a committee of central bankers. It is a pity that the proposal to set up a second committee composed of a wide spectrum of commercial and financial companies and consumer interests, advised by academic and official experts, was not followed, to act as a balance. The terms of reference of the EMI give it the opportunity to encourage the Community to implement mechanisms that will increase the use of the ecu in the transition, so, in practice, this approach could be followed.

The extent of economic union required
The emphasis in presenting the need for monetary union has, on this occasion, been placed on its importance in completing measures of the single market and providing various microeconomic gains through the having of a single currency. On previous occasions, a single currency had taken second place to locked exchange rates and the emphasis had been on the benefits to macroeconomic policy and the achievement of stability. The single market does not provide the whole of the characteristics of economic union and the negotiating parties used this opportunity to argue whether EMU required a wider collaboration in policy formation than had previously been the case. For example, it was argued that, to provide a proper union, Community competences should be extended to education, so that the Community's citizens could be assured an opportunity for high quality education wherever they chose to live in the EC. Anything less than that and the free movement of labour would be impeded.

The same argument was extended to the 'social chapter' which included wider proposals for social action both within the firm and outside. Should there be minimum levels for access to social provision? What minimum rights have to be offered for the wellbeing of people in the workplace, etc.? Here there were a number of objectors to the proposals, feeling that requirements would either harm their competitiveness or impose unsustainable budget deficits on member states which were already in difficulty. A blocking coalition was therefore established among the UK, Spain and Portugal to resist such proposals. In the Spanish and Portuguese cases it was not that they would not have wished to try to implement more generous social provision, just that they could not afford it. Hence when the cohesion fund was developed and the commitment to greater emphasis on social and economic cohesion was emphasised, the Spanish and Portuguese ended their opposition to the measures leaving the UK on its own. The price of that compromise is now becoming clear as a contribution to the Commission's proposals for a 30 per cent real expansion in the Community budget over the next five years.

Since the social chapter in the treaty had to be resolved under unanimity, the UK had the power (and, it seems, the inclination) to block further progress until it becomes clear that this chapter is beneficial to it. This it did very effectively despite the wishes of the other eleven countries. However, rather than letting the chapter lapse, which was the expected outcome, a last moment compromise was reached, that the other member states would go ahead with the social chapter on their own but that the chapter would be attached to the treaty as a separate agreement, rather than form part of it.

It remains to be seen whether a less regulated market in a number of dimensions does actually permit more flexibility and hence the ability to adjust more readily to shocks and the pressures for change, or whether it merely tends to reinforce a lower cost position rather than force a transition to higher value added production. Thus far the single market has not developed far enough to provide a test of these views but, as Ermisch (1990) has indicated, the lack of migration in the Community does suggest that regulations which raise labour costs may increase unemployment in the less advantaged parts of the Community. The expectation at present is that it will be possible at some stage, perhaps not in the too distant future, to return to a policy to which all twelve member states can agree, through a combination of experience and change in views.

The need for social and economic cohesion
A symmetric part of the negotiation covered the need to do something about the problems of the less favoured regions of the Community. Since these regions are concentrated in the lower income member states one might be forgiven for suggesting that this was part of the price for getting those countries' agreement to EMU changes which will benefit the more advantaged regions. More charitably, an increase in the equity of the growth process in Europe has been a feature of the EC treaties starting with the Treaty of Rome and has received progressive strengthening since then. To a limited extent the rationale has been that the less advantaged regions represent an underutilised resource, particularly insofar as that lack of advantage is reflected in higher than average unemployment, but it is also underutilised in the sense that many of the activities can be performed more efficiently, hence releasing resources for further production elsewhere.

Against this it is argued that the strengths of the Community come from fostering what it does best and that putting resources into supporting the inefficient will reduce the overall rate of growth. There has therefore been resistance, in Germany and the UK in particular, to expanding the Community's budget and to increasing the structural funds. Their view has been that, if the Community as a whole is successful, then some of that success will tend to filter through to all of the regions of the Community. Particularly, with the freedom for capital and labour to move, resources can move to where they can be most efficiently used. It is reasonably clear from the negotiations culminating in Maastricht that this view does not prevail in the Community as a whole at present or at least that this mechanism is insufficient.

The policy which has been confirmed is that limited funds should be used to create an infrastructure in both physical and human capital, which will give the less advantaged regions an equal opportunity to compete with the rest of the Community in the single market. The size of the additional funds implied appears to be a matter of dispute. The Commission has asked for a doubling in real terms over the period 1993-8 in its recent budget proposal. Some of the member states have reacted immediately that they had not intended an expansion in Community spending in total of the magnitude proposed. This promises a negotiation with the usual sparkle but it is already clear that, whatever the outcome, the Maastricht Treaty provides a clear gesture of support towards the less favoured regions.

This support for the regions, to try to deepen the involvement of all levels of government in the EC in the Community's processes, has been extended to creating a Committee for the Regions. Since this is advisory, like the Economic and Social Committee, this does not represent an awkward commitment to an interest group with demands on funds but a pointer to the way in which the deepening of the union could go, in weakening the relative position of the existing member states and focussing on regions with economic meaning, which may not coincide with previous political boundaries.

Taken together the Maastricht proposals provide a clear indication of the way forward for European Union. However, on the one hand they are a step in a process to what is described as 'ever closer union', since further work will be required on both the economic and political fronts if the internal market is to resemble, even remotely, the domestic markets of large federal markets like the US. While, on the other, several of the existing proposals have to prove themselves in practice, particularly monetary union, which is not only treading new ground but requires considerable effort on the part of many member states both to achieve it and make it work. Integration is an evolutionary process with steps both backwards and forwards. The Maastricht agreement represents a serious attempt to make a major step towards closer integration in which monetary union plays a major part. It presents a real opportunity to achieve a breakthrough which has eluded the Community for twenty years to make serious progress towards forming an economic and monetary union which can be expanded to include the rest of Europe if they wish and can develop their economic systems sufficiently.

3

Economic and Monetary Policy in a United Europe

The signing of the Maastricht Treaty opens up the road to EMU and a single currency before the end of this decade. The member states of the European Community have decided to follow this road for three reasons. The first is political: there is a growing belief in Europe as a cultural unity and a focus of loyalty. The second is a matter of practical convenience and economic efficiency: the use of a dozen different kinds of money is a source of inefficiency and a handicap to business. The third concerns the conduct of monetary and fiscal policy: it is widely accepted that the countries of Europe stand a better chance of achieving price stability if they tackle the problem together.

In this chapter and the next we shall try to describe not only the steps towards EMU but also how economic and monetary policy might be conducted after EMU has been achieved. This is an exercise of foresight or vision, trying to grasp how the new system will work, what its aims will be and how it will go about achieving them. It is also an exercise of interpretation, reading between the lines of the Maastricht Treaty, trying to understand what the drafters and the signatories had in mind. We need a clear idea of this ultimate destination in order to take the initial steps which will be necessary over the next few years.

Suppose then that we find ourselves some ten or fifteen years hence, in the early years of the twenty-first century. EMU has been in operation for some years and most of the initial transitional difficulties have been overcome. The ecu has replaced the national currencies of Europe; there is a European central bank which has taken over from national central banks all responsibility for monetary policy. All, or most, of the present member states of the European Community, together with a few new members, are participating in EMU — there is no need to be too specific about who is in and who is out.

In this chapter we view the scene from the centre, from the point of view of the EMU as a whole, and the institutions that are responsible for policymaking at that level. In the next chapter we shall adopt the rather different perspective of the member state and national policymakers. First, then, we consider what determines the performance of the European economy as a whole. After that we ask what prevents the economies of the individual member states from diverging away from the rest of the European Union.

The approach to economic policy which is expressed in the Maastricht Treaty has been adopted by policymakers gradually over the last two decades. It is very different from the philosophy which guided economic policy in the days when the European Economic Community was founded, different too from the views of policymakers in most countries during the 1960s and the 1970s. The theory is ultimately based on classical economics and the liberal tradition of political thought. It owes much to the re-assertion (and re-interpretation) of that tradition in the United States as well as in Europe during the 1970s and 1980s. These ideas now lie behind the day-to-day pronouncements of officials in most Western capitals, and in international organisations including the IMF, the OECD and the European Commission. We assume, in our projection to the early years of the next century, that these ideas still dominate.

This chapter is organised as follows. First we take the aim of price stability, written into the Treaty as the overriding aim of monetary policy. What will it mean in practice? Then we ask how it will be achieved. What will be the instruments of monetary policy? Will they be effective? Secondly we will consider the exchange rate of the ecu in world currency markets, against the dollar, the yen and so on. What kind of international monetary system will there be? Who will be responsible for the exchange rate policy of the European Union? Thirdly we will consider the effects of fiscal policy, the total across all member states of government borrowing. Will this be coordinated in any way from the centre? Will it be compatible with monetary stability? And, following on from that, we ask how the Union, acting as a whole, can contribute to the aims of output stability and full employment. We complete the chapter by imagining two kinds of shocks to the Union and how it may have to respond.

Price stability

In classical economics price stability is the responsibility of the monetary authorities because they control the quantity of money. The price level varies with the amount of money in circulation, originally coins made of precious metal, later bank notes and nowadays entries in bank accounts. The idea is very straightforward, but the application to a modern economy can be troublesome.

The advantage of price stability is not just that it does away with a lot of tedious calculations to compensate for the rate of inflation. The main benefit is that it is possible to enter into contracts or agreements defined in money terms, knowing that the figures in the agreement will still mean the same thing when the contract is fulfilled. This is important to business, and also to anyone who takes out life insurance or borrows on the security of their house. It would be impossible to keep the price level exactly the same each year, but price rises in one year would be offset by price falls in another, so that the level did not trend upwards from year to year. This was the typical behaviour of the price level in the period when monetary policy was constrained by the gold standard.

The experience of Europe in the last twenty years has been very different from that. The average rate of inflation in the European Community has been 8.2 per cent a year and in every year the average price level has risen. The peak was in 1974 when the European average inflation rate was over 14 per cent, and the trough was in 1986 when it was just 3.2 per cent. No member state has achieved price stability on average over those twenty years, or come anywhere near it. The best performance was in Germany where the rate averaged nearly 4 per cent, with a peak of over 7 per cent and a trough of minus per cent.

For inflation to be zero on average it may be necessary, in a typical year, for the price index to fall in half the member states. In some cases this would involve cuts in wages as well as prices. The price level on average for Europe as a whole would probably have to fall as often as it rose. But experience suggests that in a modern economy price increases tend to be permanent, and price cuts temporary.

The measurement of price stability is itself a difficult subject. The goods and services which made up the consumer price index will be different in different places, and will change from year to year. The measurement of quality is notoriously difficult; so if quality rises from year to year, as it clearly does for some (but not all) items, then price indices may slightly overstate the rate of inflation. When price stability becomes the explicit objective of monetary policy, it would be helpful to have a 'quality-adjusted' price index to hand.

The Maastricht Treaty goes to some lengths to set precise arithmetical targets for convergence, but nowhere does it define 'price stability'. In effect the central bankers will be left to define their own objectives. There is no 'anchor' tying down the price level in the long run, as there was under the gold standard. If, by accident, the price level rises in one year there is no pressure on the central bankers to bring it back down again. If the shocks to the system are asymmetrical — more often pushing prices up than down — then the price level may tend to drift slowly upwards.

The central bankers will want to set themselves targets which are possible to achieve. They will be independent of national and international governments, but they will be dependent on the support of public opinion. As public servants, they cannot be indifferent to the priorities of the people they serve. It is doubtful whether they would have much public support if they adopted targets that required frequent reductions in prices or wages, but public opinion does care about price stability. The experience of the 1970s means that all over Europe there is now widespread concern to prevent a recurrence of rapid price increases. We assume that this concern is still there when EMU is fully operational and provides the support which the central bank needs if it is to do its job effectively.

Over the past ten years the rate of inflation in Germany has averaged about 2 per cent a year. There was an actual fall in the price index in one year out of those ten. If this performance could be generalised to the whole of Europe, and maintained over several decades, then this would be a remarkable achievement and sufficiently close to price stability for most of the population. It may not satisfy the purist, but this seems to be a reasonable guess at the outcome to be achieved under EMS once the system is fully operational.

Monetary policy

With just one currency, the ecu, in use, and no restrictions of transactions between member states, there can be only one rate of interest for assets of equivalent status and maturity in all the money markets of Europe. That interest rate must be under the control of the central banking system. The way in which that control is secured is of secondary importance. At present the techniques are different in different member states, but by the time that monetary union is achieved they will have to be brought into line.

The long-term rate of interest, say the yield on 10-year government bonds, is not now under the control of the central bank in any of the member states, and it will not be an instrument of monetary policy under EMU. But, with a single currency, the yields on similar bonds will be the same in all markets irrespective of the nationality of the borrower.

If the bonds of some governments yield a higher rate than others, this will be because they have borrowed more or because they are considered to carry some risk of outright default. The European central bank will not be lending directly to the governments of any member states, and it will not be underwriting their debts. But provided that their borrowing is not thought by the markets to be 'excessive' it would be surprising if they had to pay a premium above the going-rate for public debt. An 'excessive' deficit is defined in the Treaty in a relatively strict sense, and the level of debt specified by the Treaty as a 'ceiling' is relatively low. It is likely, therefore, that some states which participate in EMU will be justifying their fiscal policy either as being transitional or temporary. This will be one means by which the central bank and member states collectively exert authority over any state that threatens to step too far out of line. It will ensure that fiscal policy is not conducted in such a way as to make monetary control more difficult.

According to classical tradition central banks ensure price stability by controlling the money supply, not by controlling interest rates. The system of monetary control under EMU will fit into that description, and it will be necessary both to define a European money supply and to establish means of controlling it. Currently numerous different definitions of the money supply (broader or narrower) exist in most member states, and it is unusual for exactly the same definitions to be used in different countries. Some central banks set monetary targets; none hit them consistently. The methods of control, or attempted control, differ among states as well. During the transition to EMU this whole apparatus of targetry will have to be overhauled. Common definitions must be established consistent with the changing methods of monetary control and banking supervision. The officials of the central bank will be confronted with a set of relatively new, and untried, statistics and operating methods. The process of financial integration itself will obscure the underlying relationships between the quantity of money and the rate of inflation. Monetary control will necessarily be a somewhat 'hit-and-miss' business during that transition and for some time after that, although this does not mean that control of inflation need be at risk.

The move to a single currency will ultimately make monetary control much easier. At present the widespread use of foreign currency in financial markets makes it difficult to gauge the demand for money of any one kind. Thus the D-Mark is used extensively outside Germany. Between now and the establishment of EMU the international use of the D-Mark, and also of the ecu, is likely to increase. In those circumstances it becomes more difficult for a national central bank to play its proper role. This problem will be solved only when a single currency replaces all others and when there is a European central bank to control it. (This is one reason to hope that the transition period to the single currency will not be too long.)

If we look ahead to the early years of the next century we can imagine the system fully adjusted, with the difficult transition made. Monetary statistics are collected in all member states on the same definition for total ecu bank deposits (the broad money supply) and also for ecu notes and coin plus bankers' balances (the narrow money supply) and maybe several variations on those themes. Attention is focussed on total notes and coin because it is thought to give the clearest indication of inflationary pressures — apart from the troublesome business of the leakage into Eastern Europe. Targets are set each year for the total growth of this narrow aggregate — and usually those targets are hit. No attempt is made to hit targets for this aggregate on a country-by-country basis, but some attention is paid to the nationality of the banks which contribute to the growth of the money supply on its broad definition.

Since the central bank does not actually ration notes and coin, control of that narrow aggregate is indirect. If the growth of the narrow money supply is excessive the central bank acts to restrain the whole financial system by raising interest rates and putting pressure on bank reserves. If this action is vigorous enough it will restrain as severely as is necessary the growth not only of the money supply, but of the price level as well.

When interest rates are raised no distinction can be made within EMU between different member states. If the total money supply, or the average price level, of Europe is rising too fast, interest rates will be raised for everyone, not just in the areas where inflationary pressure is at work. It is easy to imagine this causing a certain amount of ill-feeling from time to time. (This is not an altogether new situation: it arises now within member states and also between member states in the context of the ERM.) In the next chapter we shall discuss what action (if any) national governments might be able to take. But the central bankers might not be entirely indifferent to the way that their actions affected different member states.

Monetary control always involves a certain amount of arm-twisting as well as the more public business of setting interest rates or reserve ratios. If a situation arises, under EMU, when bank credit is known to be expanding much more rapidly in some parts of the Union than others, the central bankers will not necessarily want the Union as a whole to suffer as a result. The central bank governors of the member states involved might be asked to do something about it. They will pass the message on to the commercial banks who are contributing to the problem. An informal credit control, of a very imprecise kind, may therefore exist, although its effectiveness, especially in the more developed financial centres, must remain in doubt.

For most of the 1970s and 1980s central banks fought a relentless, but often unsuccessful, battle against inflationary expectations. When the price level is always expected to rise, it requires stern and unpopular action to hold it down. In projecting a vision forward more than ten years to a time when EMU is well established we must assume that the habit of persistent high inflation has been broken. The assumption that everyone has to have a pay increase every year no longer holds. Contracts no longer make provision for automatic indexation (even where it is legally possible to do so). In these circumstances the conduct of monetary policy becomes much easier.

EMU will not be started unless the rate of inflation is low. The change of currency emphasises the break with the past. So the system should be able to get off to a good start. In the absence of 'shocks' to the price level that performance should be maintained. We shall consider later in the chapter how it might respond if the fates are not so kind.

The exchange rate of the ecu

In an open economy one of the most direct and reliable ways in which the monetary authorities can reduce the price level is to raise the exchange rate. Under a 'fixed-but-adjustable' regime like the postwar Bretton Woods system or the exchange rate mechanism of the EMS, the exchange rate could simply be revalued. Under a floating rate system the authorities could buy their own currency in the market in an attempt to bid its price up, or alternatively they could raise interest rates to encourage inflows of capital. We do not know for certain what regime will be operating in the world monetary system in the early years of the next century, so in discussing European exchange rate policy we must look at more than one possibility.

Since 1987 the Group of Seven countries (the United States, Japan, Germany, France, Italy, Canada and the United Kingdom) have operated a system of 'reference ranges' for the dollar, the yen and the D-Mark. The original ranges have been rebased, or in effect realigned, several times, and on occasion the dollar has been allowed to stray out of its range. If the world system remains the same after EMU is formed, the ecu will take the place of the D-Mark in this tri-polar arrangement.

The question then arises as to who will be responsible for setting the reference ranges for the ecu, and for the market intervention (buying or selling ecu against dollars or yen) which may be necessary in order to stay inside them. In the Maastricht Treaty responsibility for exchange rate policy is shared between the central bank and the council of ministers, but the relative weight attached to the two voices remains uncertain, and also the means by which a conflict of views could be resolved.

The possibility of a difference of opinion should not be underestimated. The central bank will have price stability as its main objective. Sometimes that will be best served by an appreciation of the ecu against the dollar and the yen. Sometimes selling ecu to prevent the currency appreciation will add to the European money supply and conflict with the aim of domestic monetary stability. Conflicts of just this kind have been endemic in Germany, where the Bundesbank has responsibility for domestic monetary policy but not for the exchange rate.

The conflict can also be illustrated in terms of relative interest rates. Arbitrage and speculation in world currency markets will make sure that the interest differential between the ecu and the dollar is equal to the expected change in the exchange rate between them. If that were not the case capital would all rush to the currency which offered the better combination of interest plus expected appreciation. If the authorities who control the exchange rate create the expectation that the ecu will be fixed against the dollar, then interest rates must be the same in both currencies. Conversely if the central banks in Europe and the United States set different interest rates then the ecu-dollar exchange rate must 'jump' to the level where its expected future movement offsets the interest differential. The European authorities can choose either the interest rate or the exchange rate for the ecu, but not both inconsistently.

At this point some guesswork is necessary. In Europe under EMU the central banking system will be a tightly-organised entity with a clear aim and purpose. There is no suggestion of a European Finance Ministry with similar weight and authority. The likelihood must be that the central

Economic and Monetary Policy in a United Europe   45

bankers will get their way most of the time. It would be different if the G7 arrangement were more tightly defined, with overt narrow bands in place of 'reference ranges' that can shift around. The fact that four different finance minsters from Europe all attend the G7 meetings does not necessarily increase their effectiveness. In ten or fifteen years' time the international monetary system will be an equal partnership between three major 'players', the United States no longer able to exercise dominance. But the influence of Europe will be exercised by its central bankers rather than its politicians. A reasonable guess would be that the European central bank, together with the Federal Reserve Board and the Bank of Japan, will take the most important decisions. It is possible, also, that agreements about 'reference ranges' and market stabilisation will be less important under EMU than they are now. We could move back towards a more freely floating system, without necessarily abandoning intervention of a purely tactical kind to 'smooth the markets'.

If international markets believe the European commitment to price stability, then the ecu should be at least as likely to appreciate against the dollar as the D-Mark has been in the EMS. To start with, when EMU is first set up, the European Central Bank may not enjoy the same reputation for enforcing price stability as does the Bundesbank. But if all goes well that reputation will be earned in a few years once EMU is in operation. At present there is, at times, a reluctance to let the D-Mark rise against the dollar because this would be inappropriate for the other currencies tied to the D-Mark by the exchange rate mechanism. When there is just one European currency this anxiety will disappear. Provided that the level of interest rates set by the European central bank is no lower than the rate that the Bundesbank would have set in the same circumstances, the ecu will tend to be more buoyant than the D-Mark has been.

In our projection of life under EMU we could expect lower nominal interest rates in Europe than in America, associated with a better record of price stability on this side of the Atlantic, and an upward trend of the ecu against the dollar. The alternative case would be a fixed or nearly-fixed rate for the ecu against the dollar, set by negotiation between finance ministers, leading to some compromise with the objective of very low inflation.

Fiscal policy in an EMU

In classical economics government borrowing is seen as a sign of weakness, or at best as a regrettable necessity. The provisions of the Maastricht Treaty are concerned with preventing 'excessive' fiscal deficits, not with preventing 'inadequate' deficits or 'excessive' surpluses. No doubt this reflects the experience of most countries over many decades, or even centuries.

The fiscal powers of the Union as a whole will be very limited and its budget very small relative to the aggregate public spending or taxation of its member states. At present the EC's total budget is little more than 1 per cent of Community GDP. We shall consider in the next chapter what use the member state governments will make of fiscal instruments. The issue here is more one of coordination. Will the fiscal policies of member states add up to an appropriate policy for the Union as a whole? Or will the budget deficits and surpluses, motivated by different aims or circumstances, tend rather to cancel one another out?

Figures are available for average borrowing by governments of nine member states (the present twelve excluding Greece, Spain and Portugal) each year since 1960. There is an underlying trend towards larger deficits in relation to national incomes. The average deficit was   per cent in the 1960s, 3 per cent in the 1970s and 4 per cent in the 1980s. This ratio was increased sharply in the mid-1970s and has not fallen back much since then.

Around this upward trend the variation has been in the main countercyclical. Thus the years of largest deficit ratios were 1975 and 1982 when Europe was in cyclical downturn. In 1989 the ratio was down to about 2 per cent, but since then it has risen again. It is projected by the Commission at over 4 per cent for 1992. The deficits do not cancel each other out because the member states experience a common cycle of rise and fall in economic activity.

These cyclical swings result mainly from the operation of 'built-in stabilisers', such as the fall in tax revenue that accompanies a recession, or the rise in social security spending when unemployment increases. It would indeed be very difficult to suppress these 'stabilisers' since the cycle cannot easily be observed until economic statistics are available well after the event. It would also be undesirable to suppress them, as they tend to mitigate the severity of both booms and slumps.

As the European economy becomes more closely integrated, looking ahead to a point when EMU is well established, the rise and fall in output and employment will be more closely synchronised across member states. This will also amplify the cyclical variation in the figures for average budget deficits referred to above. This would be no bad thing, provided it does not conflict with the aim of preserving price stability.

A closer coordination of fiscal policy would require each member state to contribute to an overall plan for the fiscal 'stance' appropriate to the Union as a whole. This would require discretionary changes in taxation or expenditure, rather than simply the passive response of the 'built-in stabilisers'. In the past it has been argued that coordination of this kind was appropriate since each member state was otherwise constrained by the consequence of fiscal expansion for its currency or its balance of payments. But in an EMU these external constraints will not have the same significance. There will be no exchange rates between member states to worry about, and balance of payments deficits will be easier to finance,

Economic and Monetary Policy in a United Europe 47

provided they are clearly of limited duration — as they would be if they really were the result of countercyclical fiscal policy.

Clearly our picture of policymaking within EMU early in the twenty-first century should include regular meetings of finance ministers and their officials to exchange views on the state of the European economy and the fiscal policy measures they have taken since they last met. But it is doubtful whether, in normal times, those meetings would be crucially important to the conduct of policy. We shall consider below how they might react in an emergency. Perhaps more effective coordination would make such emergencies less likely — this is one area where the Maastricht Treaty has not given a very clear lead.

Where then does this leave the idea that economic policy should contribute to the aims of faster growth or full employment? There is no room for complacency on either account. The average annual growth rate of output in the twelve present members of the Community was 4.8 per cent in the 1960s, 3.0 per cent in the 1970s and 2.3 per cent in the 1980s. The rate of unemployment in the same countries was 2.3 per cent in the 1960s, 4.1 per cent in the 1970s and 9.6 per cent in the 1980s.

The achievement of a lower rate of inflation would itself help to stimulate faster growth. This would be associated with a lower nominal interest rate and hence a higher rate of investment. Price stability should lead to a better allocation of resources and a more efficient economy.

The process of closer economic integration in Europe should itself lead to greater efficiency, and to faster growth. Forming EMU is an important part of that process and will itself result in significant cost savings. The changes of institution and structure required in member states to make EMU possible, the removing of control on capital movements for example, will usually assist economic development as well.

Economics in the classical tradition would not expect that a stimulus to demand resulting from relaxing monetary or fiscal policy would add to the growth of output except in the short run. In the longer term the only effect of such a relaxation would be to raise the price level. This classical view now prevails in most central banks and finance ministries (although not always in ministries of industry or the economy). It greatly simplifies the conduct of monetary and fiscal policy, as it does away with the unpleasant dilemma they would face if long-term growth had to be sacrificed in the interests of price stability.

The classical view of unemployment is that it is caused by labour market 'rigidity', high real wages and by the generosity of social security benefits. None of these are the immediate concern of fiscal or monetary policy. It is not incompatible with this view however to recognise that the reduction of inflation almost always requires a period of slack in the labour market.

Repeated doses of this medicine have been necessary in many European countries, leading to sustained periods of high unemployment. When unemployment is high for a long time, it becomes more difficult to reduce, not least because many workers experience difficulty in finding a job after a spell of say a year or more out of work. If monetary and fiscal policy were conducted so effectively that inflation never became engrained in the economy, then the danger of such 'ratcheting' of unemployment would not arise. In the absence of adverse 'shocks' to the European economy then it is perhaps not unrealistic to hope that the level of unemployment generally will be rather lower than it is now once EMU has been operating successfully for some time.

Reactions to 'shocks'

It remains to consider what will happen to that system if surprises do happen. In particular we consider a surge of world commodity prices and a slump arising from instability in world financial markets.

The case of the commodity price surge could arise from cartelisation, which made possible the oil price rises of the 1970s, or from natural disasters, or from war. The immediate effect would be to raise the price level throughout Europe, but by differing amounts in different member states. The central bank would react to this rise in prices, but it could not react so swiftly as to prevent the rate of inflation rising in the short term. Having one monetary authority for the whole of Europe committed to price stability should make the reaction swifter and more decisive. Interest rates would be higher, but the exchange rate would be unaffected if other central banks reacted in the same way. The loss of real incomes, coupled with the higher level of interest rates would reduce aggregate demand throughout Europe (although to different degrees in different member states). If the severity of the policy tightening was nicely judged, inflation would be brought to a halt and the level of output and employment restored within a relatively short period. If not, there might be a period of 'overshooting' in which demand remained very depressed, and prices actually fell.

This kind of emergency has arisen several times in postwar history, triggered by the Korean War, the Vietnam War, the Arab-Israeli conflict and the revolution in Iran. Central bankers have had plenty of experience, and time to reflect on the mistakes of the past. If it happened again it could be a painful experience, but those responsible would know how to cope. For experience of a proper slump one has to look back to the interwar years. It is now generally recognised that central bankers, and governments, reacted at that time in altogether the wrong way. But the incident is now so remote in time that it is not so easy to learn from their mistakes.

Europe could not hope to isolate itself completely from a panic originating in America, or Japan, or elsewhere in the international financial system. Markets worldwide are even more closely linked nowadays than they were in the 1930s. Europe is also vulnerable to a fall in demand in world markets for exports of manufactured goods, or to the imposition of trade restrictions. The result could be a serious recession throughout Europe to which the central bank and national governments would have to coordinate a response. The central bankers would have to judge when their prime concern with price stability had to take second place to the safeguarding of the banking system and the preservation of adequate liquidity. Finance ministers would have to accept that the normal definition of fiscal rectitude did not apply, and that a period of exceptionally heavy public borrowing was both prudent and necessary. If action of this kind were not coordinated by the European Union, then member states might resort to individual solutions which would effectively wreck EMU. A joint response should be much better than uncoordinated or competitive actions.

In trying to foresee how EMU will work, it should not be forgotten that national governments will still be there. Political union will go forward in parallel, but on present plans it will not go very fast. National governments will still be answerable to their own parliaments and electorates. If the performance of national economies is not going well, the blame will rest, rightly or wrongly, with national governments — if only because they set the system up. If it goes well they will be able to take the credit. In the next chapter we shall look at EMU from their point of view, and in particular at the way international balance can be maintained when the countries are subject to a single monetary authority and when their currency is the same.

4

Achieving and Maintaining Convergence

As explained in Chapter 2 above, economic convergence between the members states is a precondition, in the Maastricht Treaty, for progress towards EMU. Before the second stage is introduced the degree of convergence will be assessed, especially with regard to inflation and public finance. Then before the transition to the third, and crucial, stage, the performance of each member state will be examined to see whether they are ready to participate in a monetary union. Four criteria will be used: inflation, government borrowing, exchange-rate stability and interest rates. Thus, no member state will be part of EMU unless it can satisfy the others collectively that its performance is satisfactory on all these accounts. In this chapter we consider the steps necessary to achieve convergence and also to maintain it once EMU is formed. In this chapter we concentrate on the principles involved. In Chapter 7 we shall look at the history and the prospects for each of the twelve member states in turn.

It is significant that a test of convergence should have been set which must be passed before EMU is formed. In the debate which has taken place over the years about the best path to EMU there have been two schools of thought. One argued that convergence was a necessary prior condition for monetary union, the other that establishing a monetary union was enough to ensure that convergence would take place. There is undoubtedly truth in both propositions, and both are relevant to the plans for EMU as now established. When EMU is set up the member states will be in a state of convergence and it will be essential to make sure that they do not subsequently diverge. Certainly the fact of being in a monetary union will make it much easier to avoid the risk of divergence, but the possibility raises some anxieties which need to be addressed.

Convergence means the narrowing of international differences in economic characteristics and performance. We can usefully distinguish convergence of three different kinds. Nominal convergence, that is the narrowing of differences in 'nominal' variables including cost and price inflation is a necessary property of a monetary union. Real convergence, which means narrowing the dispersion of 'real' variables like productivity and living standards is one aim of economic integration in Europe, but it is not a necessary condition for EMU. Finally, structural convergence, meaning the assimilation of economic institutions and practices, may assist convergence of both the other kinds.

Nominal convergence

In a monetary union inflation rates cannot be far out of line. Once exchange rates are fixed any country which allows its prices to rise substantially faster than the rest will lose competitiveness and market share. The move to establish a common central bank and a common monetary policy means that inflationary pressure is unlikely to differ greatly in different member states. The move to a single market means that divergences in relative prices are more likely to result in 'arbitrage' trade. And the move to a single currency will make any such divergences more obvious to the ordinary consumer.

But the rate of inflation will not always be exactly identical, since different countries will buy a rather different set of products and since some goods and services cannot easily be traded. (There is nothing in a monetary union to ensure that the price of a haircut is the same in Athens and in Edinburgh, or even that it rises at the same rate over time; but the price of a litre of petrol or a television set in the two cities cannot get far out of line.) The experience of those countries in Europe which have kept their exchange rates fixed in recent years has been that their rates of inflation stay close to one another all the time.

Before EMU is formed, it may not be thought sufficient to demonstrate that rates of inflation have been held close together for a few years, it should also be shown that they have been held together without strain. Convergence may be merely superficial. If so the strain will show in indices of relative costs, in balance of payments deficits or in unemployment. These may all be signs of imbalance which will need eventually to be corrected. One must be confident that they will be corrected within the EMU.

It is also a precondition for EMU that the fiscal balance and the stock of public sector debt should not be excessive in the prospective participants. This condition is related to that of nominal convergence. Fiscal extravagance leads in the end to inflation. It is possible to finance a reasonably large deficit by selling public sector debt to willing holders at home or abroad. Beyond a certain point governments are often forced to resort to bank finance, which adds to the money supply and threatens inflation. Historically, when governments have allowed their stock of debt to rise faster than national income (for example in wartime) there comes a point when the interest on the debt exceeds the taxable capacity of the country.

Thereafter the real value of the debt is usually eroded by inflation. To avoid any risk of this happening within EMU the Treaty puts constraints on the behaviour of any persistent debtor countries.

The Treaty also requires that participants in EMU have not recently devalued their currencies. Some commentators have suggested that there should be one last round of realignments in the exchange rate mechanism just before EMU is established to make sure that member states do not enter the system with their currencies 'misaligned'. But the main purpose of the convergence criteria is to make member states demonstrate in advance that they are able to manage without exchange rate changes. Once inside EMU there can be no more realignments. The transition to EMU would be difficult to handle if member states were all seeking to adjust their exchange rates one more time. Moreover if a country has just devalued its currency immediately before joining EMU it is very likely to add to cost pressures in that country, and as a result its rate of inflation is likely to accelerate in the difficult early years of the new system.

The criterion which requires interest rates to be approximately equal is another test of nominal convergence. Within a monetary union interest rates will be the same in all member states, because otherwise capital will flow towards the country with the highest rate, assuming there is no risk of the union breaking up. Thus the interest-rate requirement amounts to a test of the credibility of the candidate's commitment to EMU as seen by the financial markets (admittedly a rather weak one since a 2 percentage point margin is allowed). If the monetary authorities cannot convince the markets that they are in earnest about joining EMU, then they will not be allowed in.

Maintaining convergence

Let us now imagine the situation as it might be some years after EMU has been established. Continuing the exercise begun in Chapter 3 we seek to present a view of the not-very-remote future as it seems the authors of the Maastricht Treaty intend it to be. Now we shall put ourselves in the position of a national government or a member of parliament in a member state. Some anxiety has been expressed about the loss of control over monetary policy, and the difficulty of economic adjustment in member states when neither their exchange rates nor their interest rates can be changed. No doubt the system will be subject to a variety of shocks.

One kind of shock which we have already mentioned in Chapter 3 would be an increase in world commodity or oil prices. Different member states would be affected to different degrees. In the case of oil, for example, some countries consume more than others, and some are producers. The CAP isolates European agriculture to some extent from disturbance to world food markets, but to the extent that prices in Europe did rise in response to a surge in world food prices, the effects would be quite different in different member states. Many commodity price increases in the past have been associated with war, or the threat of war. As political union progresses it becomes less likely that any member states will be involved in armed conflict unless they all are. Nevertheless if a war did break out somewhere outside Europe, even assuming that European countries were not themselves involved, there would be economic repercussions which could cause inflation in some countries to a greater extent than others.

Even if the external shock had the same effect on all member states in the first instance, the price level response might be different. This was certainly true of Europe following the oil price shocks of the 1970s. In some countries the rise in oil prices was fully passed on in the prices of all goods and services, and wages were then increased in an attempt to preserve their real value. In other countries, especially after the second oil price shock, the initial effect was partly absorbed by profit margins and wages were not increased proportionately. These differences in the response to inflation reflect the different institutional arrangements for wage bargaining — institutions which may have evolved in response to the different experience of inflation in different countries in earlier years. If a similar asymmetric response occurred within EMU, then relative prices and costs in different member states could get seriously out of line.

Equally prices could get out of line for purely domestic reasons. Trade unions in one member state may press successfully for wage increases, or reductions in hours of work. There may be changes in tax rates or social security contributions. There may be large-scale migration of labour between countries, or sharp changes in the flow of capital. Some regions will prosper and others will decline. For any of these reasons, some member states may find themselves out of balance with the rest of Europe.

It will not always be possible to detect such an imbalance simply by comparing indices of relative costs or prices. These indices may diverge a little, without causing any immediate problems at all, as a result of different trends in productivity growth or simply the different composition of goods each country produces and consumes. The symptoms of imbalance will be found in the trade statistics. If costs get out of line then some countries will be gaining market share, within Europe and also in world markets, whilst others will be falling behind. If that trend continued it would be necessary to correct it.

When such an imbalance occurs between countries under a flexible exchange rate system, a realignment or a market adjustment will sometimes, but not always, help to correct it relatively quickly. Not always, because quite often the imbalance will recur as inflation accelerates in the country which has devalued. When an imbalance occurs between regions of a single country, it will be offset to some degree by fiscal transfers. The regions where costs are too high will become poorer, so they will pay less taxes and receive more social security benefits. This transfer will make the imbalance easier to tolerate, but will do nothing to correct it. But within EMU there will be neither exchange rate changes nor large-scale fiscal transfers. How, then, will the system respond?

According to classical economics international balance is maintained by the flow of gold. Suppose that prices are too high, exports are uncompetitive and the country has a deficit on the balance of payments. In the days of the gold standard the net flow of goods and services into the country would be paid for by a net flow of gold in the opposite direction. As the stock of gold in the country was gradually run down, the quantity of money would fall, and so in due course would the level of prices. When prices had fallen far enough, international competitiveness would be restored, the international accounts would be restored to balance and the flow of gold would stop.

A similar mechanism can operate in a modern economy, although the gold standard is no longer observed. If the residents of one country are running a financial deficit with the rest of the world, that deficit must still be matched by a flow of capital in some form. The residents must be running down their assets in some way or increasing their indebtedness to the rest of the world. This is just as true with a monetary union as it is between countries with their own currencies. Under EMU the flows may not be so easy to observe, but they will be taking place just the same.

Gradually the drain of net assets from the high cost country will reduce the spending by its residents. That will reduce the volume of imports and release resources for the production of more exports, so that international balance will gradually be restored — a process which could take some years to complete. Thus the flow of net wealth plays a role rather similar to that of gold in the classical tradition, but the cost ratio is not necessarily restored even when the adjustment is complete. The residents of the high-cost economy end up poorer as the result of their over-spending (or the over-spending of their government).

In fact relative price changes are still essential to full adjustment between countries, within an EMU or any other system. In addition to the flow of financial assets between countries, there is an adjustment mechanism caused by changes in output and employment. In a high-cost economy output and employment will fall, because firms will produce less if demand is depressed, and because some firms will shift production abroad. Spare capacity and unemployment will slow down wage and price inflation, gradually bringing international competitiveness back into line. This process may, in fact, correct the balance of payments deficits more rapidly than the asset-flow mechanism described above. What it required, of course, is 'flexibility' of wages and prices, that is to say a rapid — and therefore relatively painless — response to a reduction in the pressure of demand.

For completeness we should also mention the possibility of labour migration as a method of international adjustment. Within nation states, for example the United States of America, migration on a significant scale occurs from relatively depressed to relatively prosperous regions. Migration between member states of the European Community is important for labour markets in Spain, Greece, Ireland and Portugal, and parts of other countries, but mainly as a result of persistent differences in levels of real income. As a means of coping with imbalances resulting from temporary disturbances to relative costs it is expensive and inefficient. It is no substitute for the necessary flexibility of relative pay and prices in each member state.

Wage and price flexibility

The term 'flexibility' in this context should not be misunderstood. If wages are rapidly adjusted up in response to a shock to the price level, that may be a sign of *real* wage *in*flexibility. What is meant is an early and appropriate adjustment of wages to restore full employment. This may take place either as a result of decentralised bargaining between individual employers and employees, or as a result of bargaining which is coordinated at the national level and conducted with the national interest in mind. There are examples of both centralised and decentralised bargaining in Europe, and no clear evidence that one is better than the other.

Decentralised bargaining focuses on the situation of the individual firm. If its costs are out of line with those of its international competitors this will often be abundantly clear to both sides of the bargain. The workers, or their representatives, will be able to see that the security of their jobs depends on a 'realistic' settlement. If all firms were engaged in international trade, and if all markets were keenly competitive then perhaps we could rely on rational self-interest to ensure that international imbalances within EMU would be quickly corrected.

The problems arise when the threat of international competition is not perceived by the individual firm. An extreme case would be wage bargaining in the public sector, where the threat of competition from abroad may seem very remote indeed. Yet public sector pay may affect the aspirations of workers in the private sector as well. In all but the smallest of member states there is a relatively large part of the private sector which serves a mainly local market. If prices in that sector get out of line they will raise the cost of living for workers in the tradeable-goods sector and cut into the profit margins of exporters. An easy correction of international imbalances requires that the trend of national competitiveness is taken into account in *all* wage bargaining.

It is of prime importance therefore that everyone understands the significance of a fixed exchange rate system and the consequences of participation in EMU. The coordination of wage bargaining by national organisations of employers and trade unions, as takes place in Germany, certainly provides a good opportunity to ensure that the message is heard. Even with bargaining decentralised, national organisations (as in Belgium) can play an important role by informing their members of the national implications of their individual actions. The existence of different systems of bargaining entails different distributions of the onus for action.

The existence of national minimum wages provides another opportunity for ensuring an appropriate response. The level and rate of change of the minimum wage may have a greater or lesser effect on the level and rate of change of wages more generally. The extent of that influence is controversial, and no doubt differs in different member states. But there is no doubt that in setting that minimum the national government, or 'social partners' at the national level, can send a clear signal of the level of settlements needed to achieve or maintain convergence of inflation with the rest of Europe at a sustainable level of costs.

Underlying this whole issue of signalling is the credibility of the EMU itself. Classical economics is founded on the assumption of rational behaviour. Rational economic agents when setting wages and prices will have to form a view of the viability and durability of the new system. If they are certain that EMU is here to stay they will change their behaviour to fit in with it. If they are doubtful, because governments seem half-hearted about it or because they remember earlier disappointments, then they will stick to their old ways of doing things. In this respect the introduction of the ecu as a single currency, replacing the old national ones, will provide the clearest possible signal that a new regime has begun.

The role of national governments

The immediate challenge to national governments and central banks is to achieve a smooth transition to EMU within the timetable suggested in the Maastricht Treaty. A great deal remains to be done and the success of the venture depends on the consistency and skill of national economic policy for the rest of this decade.

When EMU is established, however, the role of national authorities is different, and in some respects diminished. Responsibility for price stability will rest, as we have indicated, with the European central banking system. But that duty cannot be discharged unless the governments of the member states, who are answerable to the voters, give the central banking system and its objectives their unqualified support. When differences of view arise governments must accept that, so far as monetary policy is concerned, the central bankers have the last word.

Outside the area of monetary policy, national governments will remain the principal actors. Their actions will be coordinated to an increasing extent, and will be taken within a framework of international agreements. But they will still be busy doing things; and if the economies of member states do not prosper, it is national governments which will have to answer for the mistakes that they have made.

Elsewhere in this book we discuss the coordination of industrial policies, competition policies, and policies towards the labour market. Our concern here is still with policies which help to achieve or to maintain convergence, so that EMU can work well. This means that we are concerned mainly with what are called 'macroeconomic' rather than 'microeconomic' policies. But the distinction may become less clearcut. Policy changes which are normally classed as 'microeconomic' may be necessary so that 'macroeconomic' policies can do their job effectively.

Fiscal policy in member states

National governments will retain responsibility for fiscal policy, that is for the level and structure of public spending and taxation, and for the size of the surplus or deficit of the public sector. The Treaty requires that borrowing should not be 'excessive', indicates how that term will be defined, and sets out the procedure which will be followed so as to ensure that member states who borrow too much have to mend their ways. In effect any government which is borrowing more than 3 per cent of national income must show good cause for doing so.

This requirement, and the related restriction on the size of debt outstanding, goes beyond what most governments would think was strictly necessary to maintain 'sound finance'. Clearly prudence requires that governments never run risks with their long-term solvency or their short-term liquidity, and the constraints of the protocol to the Maastricht Treaty should be more than adequate to prevent that happening. One reason for this extra degree of caution may be the fear that a spendthrift government, free of anxiety about its currency, will try to borrow more than its fair share of the market for ecu-denominated debt.

Whatever the motive the 3 per cent limit will constrain significantly the use of fiscal policy. In 1991 net borrowing by general government exceeded 3 per cent in all member states except Denmark, France, Luxembourg, and the United Kingdom. The average deficit across all twelve member states was 4.3 per cent. In 1992 it is expected that Germany will reduce its deficit below the 3 per cent mark, but the United Kingdom will be crossing the line in the other direction. We should expect, when EMU is well established, that the existence of this Treaty agreement will be a factor of some importance in the fiscal policy decisions of individual member states. Their autonomy will be much reduced.

We have already considered in Chapter 3 how the European Union as a whole would respond to shocks, whether to the price level or to the level of economic activity. In both cases it would be important that the responses of fiscal policy in the various member states were consistent with one another, and also that the response of member states collectively was consistent with the monetary policy of the central banking system. Again this requirement limits the scope for independent action.

We need to consider, however, the way that national fiscal policy could be used in response to shocks which are peculiar to one member state and to achieve objectives for the stability of economic activity which may be different in different countries. The use of fiscal policy for this purpose belongs to the Keynesian rather than the classical tradition of economics, but few economists of any persuasion would deny that cutting taxes or raising public spending will usually add to economic activity in the short run. Indeed the short-term effect of such a stimulus may be greater in a monetary union that it otherwise would be, because the rate of interest in a monetary union will not rise so as to offset the increase in demand. It remains doubtful whether fiscal expansion can add to output or employment in the long run, but for the purpose of smoothing out fluctuations that does not matter.

The problems with using fiscal policy for output stabilising are of a practical kind. Unlike interest rates, tax rates and public spending cannot normally be changed at frequent intervals; most countries reckon that one Budget a year is enough. So if the level of activity becomes inadequate or excessive it may be nearly twelve months before anything can be done to correct it. By then the time for action may have passed.

To this must be added the difficulty of economic forecasting. Action to stabilise activity will only be appropriate if the government can foresee the timing and amplitude of the cycle. Otherwise it will be all too easy to take action in the trough of the cycle, intended to assist the recovery but in fact prolonging the next boom. Experience suggests that forecasts, although they contain useful information, are not always a reliable guide to the strength (or even the direction) of action that is appropriate at Budget time. No doubt the situation is different in different member states and some will find fiscal stabilisation more worthwhile than others. But it would be wrong to expect too much from it anywhere.

This leaves the 'built-in' stabilisers which were mentioned in Chapter 3 — the way that taxes automatically rise in booms and fall in slumps, and the way that social security spending is linked to the level of employment. These play a useful part in offsetting country-specific shocks as well as those which affect the European Union as a whole. Indeed the question might be asked whether tax and expenditure systems should not be designed with the deliberate intention of making the system more stable. This would, in effect, remove the need for discretionary changes in tax or spending in response to the cycle, so that fiscal policy would not be so dependent on the calendar, or on forecasting judgement.

This is a matter for governments in each member state to consider in the light of their priorities and national institutions. But the existence of EMU may influence that consideration in one respect at least. Suppose that one country's economic cycle is out of phase with the rest, with unemployment rising steeply. Suppose also that its Budget deficit is already at, or beyond, the 3 per cent boundary. To announce a tax cut in those circumstances might produce frowns of disapproval from other member states or from the central banking system. The same budget deficit, resulting 'automatically' as a consequence of unchanged tax rates and spending plans, would perhaps be received with more sympathy.

A fiscal system, automatic or discretionary, which helps to stabilise activity will also, as a rule, help to preserve nominal convergence. A boom in one country causes costs to rise out of line with the rest, and a slump in one country will leave costs too high elsewhere in Europe. So ironing out the wrinkles in output will often also make EMU function better.

But there will sometimes be cases where international adjustment requires a period of cooling off in one country, and it would be a mistake for the government in that country to take fiscal action which prevented or delayed the adjustment. As explained above, when costs in one country are too high relative to the others a period of slow growth, even perhaps a recession, may be necessary to bring them back into line. The government, if it is adept enough in its use of fiscal policy, could decide between a long and shallow recession or a short and deep one, but it cannot avoid the need for adjustment altogether.

Departures from full employment are always regrettable, and long periods of high unemployment are socially as well as economically disastrous. If EMU works well then no country should face this prospect. Nevertheless unemployment is now very high in some member states, and it is quite likely that EMU will go ahead towards the end of the decade with unemployment on average still much too high, and possibly still rising. Unless that situation is put right, EMU may be blamed, rightly or wrongly, for the situation and lose popular support. The responsibility for restoring full employment will in fact rest mainly with member states.

Restoring full employment

In the mid-1960s the rate of unemployment of the twelve present members of the European Community averaged 2 per cent, the highest rates being around 5 per cent in Italy, Ireland and Greece. The far-reaching social and institutional changes which have happened in Europe since then may mean that an appropriate definition of full employment now would not be quite as comprehensive as that. The rate of unemployment in 1990 was about 5 per cent in (West) Germany, and also in the United States. It would perhaps be a realistic aim to achieve a similar percentage to that in all member states participating in EMU.

The reasons for the upward trend in unemployment in most countries in Europe are not well understood, and views differ as to the appropriate cure. It may indeed be right for different policies to be adopted in different member states, given their very different history, institutions and structure of employment. A general increase in the rate of growth of the EC's markets offers the most straightforward solution that may indeed emerge. But two issues need to be addressed in relation to all member states.

The first concerns training. Most of the unemployed are unskilled, or have skills which are no longer in sufficient demand. There is often a 'mismatch' in the labour market, such that some kinds of labour are in short supply even when unemployment is very high. This situation occurs especially in countries which are going through a rapid transition, such as will be associated with the process of European integration and market liberalisation. It occurs also in countries where vocational training is not well developed, perhaps because of an inadequate grounding in education at school. If this is the diagnosis then more resources should be devoted to retraining the unemployed. But action is also needed to improve the initial training of all new entrants to the labour market, so that they do not share the unhappy experience of their predecessors.

The second issue concerns assistance to the unemployed, both in maintaining their living standards and in looking for work. One explanation of the persistence of high unemployment is that workers who are out of a job for a long time become in effect unemployable if only because potential employers are reluctant to take them on. This has been identified as a problem requiring special attention by the Community as well as by individual member states. It could result in a 'ratchet' effect, such that an economic downturn or recession, necessary perhaps to combat inflation, leaves a legacy of high unemployment that cannot be corrected even when the danger of inflation is past. If this is the explanation then policies need to focus on the treatment of individual workers who become unemployed, providing both help and the incentive to obtain another job soon.

This 'ratchet' theory also has a clear implication for policy more generally. The costs of disinflation are serious and long-lasting. The moral is that inflation should never be permitted to rise so substantially that those costs have to be incurred. Public confidence in the central banking system is essential to achieving that end. But the way in which the preservation of price stability is approached 'at the grass roots' will vary from country to country. In some it may involve more than just the sharing of information and exhortation to observe moderation in setting wages and prices. In the appropriate institutional setting national governments, with the help of national organisations of employers and employees, may seek to build a political consensus in favour of price stability, without distorting the market determination of wage and price relativities. That consensus will depend in the first instance on recognising the independence and the determination of the European central banking system, but also on recognising the consequences for unemployment if that determination is ever put to the test.

Structural convergence

The foundation of EMU is conditional on *nominal* convergence but not necessarily on either *real* convergence or *structural* convergence. But both real and structural convergence would have advantages for the operation of EMU.

By *real* convergence we mean reduction in the dispersion of real variables, including output per head and living standards and perhaps unemployment rates. This has political implications as well as economic. The poorer member states will only be willing participants in EMU if they believe that they will prosper better inside the union than outside. The experience of closer and more frequent contact between nationals of member states as a result of EMU may make the poor countries more conscious of their relative position. The issue is one of cohesion, which is discussed in Chapter 5.

But real convergence is likely to be accompanied by structural convergence, that is a growing similarity in patterns of production and consumption, as well as institutional changes which bring member states more closely into line.

Differences in the structure of production or consumption lie behind many of the conflicts of interest that will have to be resolved in the running of EMU. Some member states are oil producers; some are more reliant than others on coal or nuclear power. The share of agriculture in employment is a good indicator of attitudes to the CAP. Natural resource endowments will remain the same, but there are other structural differences which result from the history of development in member states and from the policies pursued in the past. The liberalisation of trade, and its encouragement by EMU, may in some cases result in greater specialisation leading to greater differences in structure, but in others to similarities resulting from a common environment. For monetary policy structural convergence is helpful if it means that the different countries will respond in the same way to shocks — in particular to those which involve changes in the prices of food, fuel and raw materials.

The convergence of institutions may also occur as the natural counterpart of closer economic integration. Firms in one country will imitate the successful strategies of firms elsewhere. Different models of economic behaviour will be in competition. But equally there will be more scope for cooperation between firms in different countries if they all work to a common 'standard' — just as common standards help to remove market barriers for trade in goods or services.

So far as macroeconomic policy is concerned the main institutional issues concern financial markets and labour markets. A successful monetary policy, and the maintenance of price stability for Europe as a whole, requires that, in these two areas, the economic system is working well in all the member states of EMU. It is helpful if it works everywhere on broadly similar lines. Financial markets are essential to the operation of monetary policy. The central banking system will need to be confident of controlling interest rates, and the growth of credit and liquidity, throughout the Union. Moreover the free movement of capital makes it necessary that the regulation of financial markets is to a similar standard everywhere.

The development of financial institutions in the past has been on rather different lines in different countries, partly as a result of different tax systems. The pattern of corporate borrowing favours equity in some countries, debt in others; and the involvement of banks and pension funds also varies a great deal. Different proportions of housing tenure result in different arrangements for lending by banks to households.

All these institutional differences mean that the response in different countries will be different to the same rise in interest rates. An increase which will be barely enough to slow down credit growth in one country may result in widespread bankruptcy and recession in another. This is not a happy situation for the European central banking system. It will have an interest in encouraging assimilation of financial institutions.

Similarly the behaviour of labour markets will determine how much unemployment rises, and how soon wage growth slows down, in each member state when the same monetary squeeze is applied to the whole European economy. Some countries have more wage flexibility; others more flexibility of employment. Some have tight regulation of hours and conditions of work; others leave such matters to be decided by the market and collective bargaining. Some have effective minimum wage laws; others do not. Without entering the debate over which of these arrangements is to be preferred, one can recognise a case on macroeconomic grounds for attempting to move closer to a common pattern. This is one justification for the social charter, which is accepted by eleven of the twelve member states.

Conclusion

We referred to the old debate about which comes first, convergence or monetary union. The answer must be that convergence begins before monetary union takes place, but continues thereafter. If one looks ahead to a period when EMU is in full operation, we do not find that all change and development has come to an end. It is not necessarily a utopia in which further improvement is impossible. Evolution will continue, leading to a convergence of structure reflecting experience. The institutions which work well under EMU will become the norm for Europe as a whole.

5

Cohesion and Economic and Monetary Union

If the transition to EMU is to succeed, all the member states need to feel they are getting something out of the move to 'European Union'. Some of them will undoubtedly endure difficulties as they seek to fulfil the conditions of convergence to enter Stage 3 of monetary union and to offset that they require sufficient appreciation that there are either offsetting benefits from other aspects of the Maastricht Treaty or that there is no viable alternative policy which would offer better results. In the main the problem comes because the member states with the greatest transition problems, Greece, Portugal and to a lesser extent Spain and Italy, are also the countries which have the regions with the lowest GDP per head and highest unemployment in the Community. The major exception is Ireland, which has actually been rather successful in meeting the conditions for convergence, as discussed in Chapter 7, but has both a relatively low income per head and high unemployment.

The high inflation member states wish to bring down inflation. If they were not in the EC they would still face the same problem. The two major differences are, first, that in seeking convergence one of the conditions is exchange-rate stability with the rest of the Community, which might be a restraint increasing the unpleasantness of the transition and, second, that they would not receive such generous support from the other member states in improving their infrastructure, assisting problems of transition, and from other Community programmes. As democracies, it is not just the economic assessment of the net benefit which will determine how they respond but the political judgement, which may involve a large number of other factors, including local rivalries and other items largely unrelated to the EC as such. How much economic support is required to help ensure this political consensus to continue to support the Community's programme of progress to European Union cannot readily be defined and may vary considerably from one region to the next.

The starting point is clearly promising, as surveys of popular opinion in the member states show a healthy majority in favour of membership and of the programmes being undertaken. It is only in Denmark and, to a lesser extent, the UK that numbers opposing EC measures have been sufficiently large to pose a serious threat, although in the early days of the previous Greek government there was substantial talk of some form of withdrawal. Nevertheless the EC does not and, indeed, will not in the immediate future, provide the sorts of assistance to less favoured parts of the Community that would be expected if the EC were a federal nation like the US, Canada or Australia. The hope of many in those regions is that it will at least make substantial moves towards that position and this is enshrined in the preamble to the Maastricht Treaty set out in the table on page 23.

One of the crucial areas of difference between the European Communities from most nation states, both at present and as planned under EMU, is in the degree of income equalisation among its regions. Depending upon how regions are defined and income per head is measured the disparities are between two and five times as great as those in the United States, West Germany and Switzerland. The main reason comes from the divergences in average incomes among the member states themselves and the lack of any budgetary mechanism to redistribute incomes among them on anything but a minor scale.

In nation states the public tax and expenditure system accounts for between around 20-40 per cent of national income and acts as a major redistributor of incomes from the rich to the poor, both in terms of households and regions. In their study of experience in a wide range of countries in the mid-1970s, the MacDougall study group, which investigated the role of public finance in European integration, noted that 40 per cent of the interregional discrepancies in incomes per head before tax were removed, on average, by the public finance system after tax. The European Communities' total budget only amounts to 1.2 per cent of Community GDP and could not hope to have such a sweeping effect. The study group's report (MacDougall, 1977) estimated that in the then Community of nine a budget of about 5-7 per cent of GDP would be needed to reduce EC regional disparities in a similar manner, although in a transitional period a budget of perhaps 2 per cent might be sufficient.

Since then the Community has expanded to include Greece, Spain and Portugal, adding considerably to the disparities. Furthermore there has been little closing of the gap over the intervening years so the demands on the Community budget would be even greater if the gap were to be closed by 40 per cent now. In any case the Community makes no attempt to reduce disparities by fiscal transfers. Its regional policy is based on the principle of trying to provide an equal opportunity for the disadvantaged regions to compete in the single market by investing in the physical infrastructure and in human skills. About a quarter of the Community's spending goes on this area, representing less than 0.3 per cent of Community GDP. The Community's budget grows only slowly and although major switches in its composition could be envisaged over the next few years there is no way that an extension of existing policies could come anywhere near reducing disparities to the scale prevalent in nation states, let alone to the lower levels of disparities that they have.

The important question, therefore, is whether this different approach matters. Just because nation states operate in this manner there is no direct reason to believe that EMU in the EC could not function properly if it failed to do the same. Whether or not real disparities between regions are important is largely a matter of their acceptability to the people involved. It is a matter of equity as much as it is a matter of economic efficiency.

The Community recognises this by treating its policies in this respect as being a matter of social and economic 'cohesion'. Cohesion, like so many aspects of Community language, is not explicitly defined but it can reasonably be interpreted (see NIESR, 1991) as the degree to which existing disparities and the attempts being made to reduce them are politically acceptable to the member states. Thus the setting of any absolute criteria in terms of percentage differentials would not define the necessary outcome, which can vary both from one part of the Community to another and as time passes. For this reason the treatment of cohesion formed an integral part of the discussions at Maastricht and its role has been considerably enhanced in the ensuing treaty. As the Delors Report itself states (p. 22), 'If sufficient consideration were not given to regional imbalances, the economic union would be faced with grave economic and political risks'.

The importance of cohesion and real convergence as a precondition for monetary union

Not all member states hold an optimistic view of how limited a measure of real convergence is required for EMU to be completed. In his contribution to the Delors Committee, Maurice Doyle, Governor of the Irish Central Bank, wrote:

It is crucial that the important *preconditions* of EMU be recognized at the outset. The process of economic integration requires a number of distinct stages, with monetary union, involving irreversibly fixed exchange rates, being the final stage. Before this can be achieved, all Community countries will need to have reached a broadly similar stage of economic development and be committed to broadly similar economic policies. If this is not the situation, disparities within the Community would cause persistent capital and labour flows from the less prosperous to the richer regions, creating both economic and political tensions that could put the whole process in jeopardy. (Delors, 1988, p.70, emphasis in original.)

Thus, completely contrary to the view expressed in *One market, one money*, that the freeing of labour and capital markets would allow the benefits from EMU to flow out to all regions of the Community, Doyle's fear is that it will deepen disparities. He has an obvious example from Irish history on his side, where, as pointed out by Bradley and Whelan (1992), it has been widely argued that economic and monetary union with Great Britain led to a progressive decline in Ireland's relative position (the industrialised part of Northern Ireland excepted) in a cycle of cumulative causation, as British competitive advantage was continously reinforced.

Taken simply, this argument runs (see Kaldor, 1971, in the context of UK membership of the EC) that if the initial adjustment process is positive, it sets in motion a virtuous circle of increased profitability for firms, enabling increased investment and R&D, which in turn brings new products and more efficient production, which enables a further gain in profitability and rise in real wages, and so on indefinitely. On the contrary, those regions requiring a downward adjustment to achieve convergence, that starts with a period of deflation and profits squeeze, can get themselves locked in a downwards spiral by an inversion of the same logic. With freedom of movement of labour and capital, both are attracted by the regions of higher returns, and because of the imperfections in the system and the dynamic nature of the gains, these flows are not sufficient to equalise the position and bring the divergence to a halt. Even the Delors Report concludes (p. 22): 'Historical experience suggests ... that in the absence of countervailing policies, the overall impact on peripheral regions could be negative'. Transport costs and economies of scale would tend to favour a shift in economic activity away from less developed regions, especially if they were at the periphery of the Community, to the highly developed areas at the centre. The economic and monetary union would have to encourage and guide structural adjustment which would help poorer regions catch up with the wealthier ones.

As O'Donnell (1991) has pointed out, these cumulative causation theories are not totally substantiated by experience, as there are plenty of examples where there has been progressive real convergence of countries in conditions where barriers are being reduced. Thus divergence is something which can occur and there are good examples from the developing world where countries have been unable to break out from their relative deprivation. However, it is also clear that such cumulative causation can be offset. In NIESR (1991) we argue that the pressures of the 1990s, from the single market, adjustment towards monetary union, the dramatic changes in central and eastern Europe and elsewhere make it likely that the adverse pressures on the 'peripheral' regions of Europe will increase during the next decade. Since many of these pressures are imposed by the EC's own desire for closer integration we, therefore, emphasise the importance of action by the Community to offset them. The New Guidelines for Community Regional Policy, issued in 1977, make exactly the same point. 'It is ... an illusion to hope for the convergence of Member States' economies so long as regional problems continue to weigh so heavily on certain economies... It follows from this ... that Community regional policy must be strengthened showing that this problem appears to be a persistent feature of European integration.'

What can the Community's policy achieve for cohesion?

In the same way that the economic debate reported in O'Donnell (1991) offers a number of conflicting paradigms about whether economic development is inherently convergent or divergent, the debate about what can be achieved by regional policy is also rather negative in its conclusions. It is now generally accepted that income transfers to disadvantaged regions achieve relatively little and may actually reinforce the causes of disparity by creating a culture of dependence in the receiving regions. At the same time the need for such transfers creates resentment in the providing regions, as witnessed by the rise of the *leghe* in Northern Italy for example, and may blunt the very sources of growth for the Community as a whole, which EMU is intended to unleash. Hence, the focus of policy tends to be on fostering the sources of indigenous growth by providing the necessary resources to develop them, through investment in infrastructure, communications, training, and so on.

The Community's structural policy is administered through three funds, the European Regional Development Fund (ERDF), the European Social Fund (ESF) and the guidance section of the agricultural funds (EAGGF), which have been organised jointly since a major reform in 1988. That reform was aimed at trying to improve the very limited impact that the previous expenditure on the structural funds had had in closing the gap in GDP per head. It had three main components, the first was a doubling of the funds available, in real terms, over the years 1988-93, the second, a focussing on the regions with the greatest disadvantages and the third, a change from assessing what to do on a project-by- project basis across the Community, to agreeing a concerted framework of action over a number of years. These changes have only been in place for a few years and the initial doubling of the funds will only be completed next year. It is therefore premature to provide a comprehensive assessment of the success and potential for this policy.

It is, however, possible to explore most of its aspects, as we have done in NIESR (1991). Unfortunately, there has been no careful assessment made of the possible success of measures designed to increase the infrastructure of a region and the concern of the member states over this is reflected in the clause of the protocol on economic and social cohesion which reads that the signatories

'REAFFIRM the need for a thorough evaluation of the operation and effectiveness of the Structural Funds in 1992.'

Doubt has been cast on the extent of benefits which stem from improving the transport infrastructure but it is clear from assessments of the determinants of inward investment (see Nam *et al.*, 1991) that the quality of the infrastructure and the local workforce are important. They are not, however, the only ones. In the opinion of Nam et al. the changes involved in the implementation of the single market will actually worsen the attractiveness of most of the least favoured regions of the Community. The main reason given is that the removal of barriers, both to easy transport and to access to public sector, means that it is no longer necessary to site inefficiently small plants in 'peripheral' areas, purely to be able to sell in them effectively. Production will be reorganised more on the basis of efficiency and will tend to gravitate towards the 'core' regions, where the network of business services is better and where delivery times are shorter and more reliable. In so far as there are further economies of scale to be exploited, they will emphasise the need for this concentration.

There are, however, two clear signs of hope. In the first place Nam et al. find that the prospects for traditional industrial areas that are in decline are actually improved by the development of the single market. These regions form the second objective of the EC's structural policy after the least favoured regions (see table 1). The reason put forward is that these regions tend not to be peripheral and, as the result of a long tradition of production, have the infrastructure, skills and business networks available for the new industries to draw on. Secondly, there has been some success from the coordination of local government, firms, educational and research institutions and financial intermediaries in creating 'islands of innovation' within Europe (Camagni, 1991). The best known of these successes is the Rhone-Alpes region in France.

Considerable improvements can be made to the operation of the existing policy in the Community by focussing on the projects which are likely to give best rates of return, by tightening up the assessment, monitoring and evaluation procedures, simplifying some of the procedures, increasing the involvement of the social partners and increasing the technical assistance available, including administrative assistance. These measures will help and extending the focus of the policy to include urban problems and the problems of migrants will increase the contribution which can be given to alleviating the costs of change. Increasing the range of instruments available to include education and health and the training of those already in work could also improve the effectiveness of this approach. The protocol on economic and social cohesion acknowledges this and the parties

'DECLARE their intention of allowing a greater margin of flexibility in allocating financing from the Structural Funds to specific needs not covered under the present Structural Funds regulations'

Nevertheless there are clear decreasing returns. On the one hand it has not been possible for some regions to take up all the assistance available. In part this problem of absorption is caused by lack of administrative capacity but it is also because of limits to suitable projects. For the least favoured regions, although the total sums involved may be small, the

Community actually contributes up to 30 per cent of the relevant categories of investment and for Ireland, Portugal and Greece, contributes up to 3-5 per cent of GDP. Since Community involvement is designed to increase total spending on this type of project in the region by at least the size of the Community's funds employed (the principle of additionality) and the member states have to contribute to them as well, usually on at least a 50-50 basis, the scope for increase is clearly limited. Again, however, the treaty protocol has something to offer to ease the constraint as the signatories

'DECLARE their willingness to modulate the levels of Community participation in the context of programmes and projects of the Structural Funds with a view to avoiding excessive increases in budgetary expenditure in the less prosperous Member States.'

The problem is clearly greatest for less favoured regions which lie in member states which themselves have a considerably below average GDP per head. This means Greece, the Irish Republic, Portugal and parts of Spain. Corsica and the French overseas territories, Southern Italy, Northern Ireland and the former East Germany all lie within member states with average or above average GDP per head. It is therefore within the powers of those member states to solve the problems of income redistribution within their territories if they wish. Much emphasis has been placed on the principle of 'subsidiarity' - responsibility for executing policy should, where possible, be assigned to the member state rather than the Commission, if this is efficient and does not result in substantial spillover effects - in the inter-governmental conferences and at Maastricht, to try to prevent 'an ever closer union' also meaning 'an ever more centralised union'. Applying this more strongly to structural policy could place more of the onus on the states with the fiscal capacity to solve their own problems.

Indeed the new cohesion fund, which was set up at Maastricht, for 'projects in the fields of environment and trans-European networks', although reportedly small in size, clearly shows this intention, as it applies to less favoured regions in member states, whose average GDP per head does not exceed 90 per cent of that of the Community as a whole — this criterion is met only by Greece, the Irish Republic, Portugal and Spain (see table 2). (The same clause also adds the requirement that the member state must be implementing a programme aimed at achieving convergence for Stage 3 to be eligible.) The major effect of this change is to eliminate the South of Italy from the calculations.

The Mezzogiorno has been receiving structural funds of one form or another for thirty years from the Community with only a limited effect on its GDP per head in many regions. There are exceptions. Abruzzi, which lies on the border, seems to have made the transition from the 'South' to the 'North' of Italy and Puglia, the next region further South along the Adriatic coast, also seems to be making considerable progress. Worries about the extent of the illegal syphoning off of funds in parts of Southern Italy are said to be a major reason why the MacDougall Report, setting out how a system of Community-wide fiscal transfers might work, was not implemented.

Reducing the scale of the problem to be addressed at the Community level could make a major contribution to its tractability. It will, at the same time, improve the chances of being able to do more for the nominal convergence of Greece, the Irish Republic, Portugal and Spain, as an increase in the funds going to them will enable the pressure on their budgets and the need to raise further debt to fall, with the potential to help in the reduction of inflationary pressure as well.

A second source of assistance to the less favoured regions has become available during 1991. As part of the European Economic Area agreement between the Community and the EFTA countries, a fund is to be set up to provide assistance from EFTA to the less favoured regions. The argument is that the effective expansion of the single market to the EFTA countries affords them access to the whole market, so they should contribute a part of the costs that this access imposes on less favoured locations. Two of the EFTA countries, Sweden and Austria, have also applied for full membership of the EC and Finland is likely to do so later this year, possibly followed by Norway and Switzerland (and presumably Lichtenstein) at a later date. This will increase the resources available for transfers and structural assistance in the Community, since all of these countries have a GDP per head well above the Community average.

In a purely technical sense, adding above average income countries to the EC will tend to worsen the relative position of the least favoured regions, as the average against which their incomes per head are calculated will rise. However, given the relatively small size of the EFTA countries compared with the rest of the Community, this will not exacerbate the problem by bringing in any large string of regions, now at the margin, into the category of being less favoured and it will not make any other country eligible for assistance under the 90 per cent rule.

It thus seems, even under the existing policy framework, that quite a lot can be done, between now and 1997-9, to ease the difficulties of the less favoured regions of the Community and improve their competitive prospects within the European single market. However, it would be a mistake to think that the Maastricht agreement marks the end of the pressure by the 'Southern' countries to improve the funds available to them as part of what they see as a quid pro quo, for the single market and other measures which tend to favour other parts of the Community rather more. The major opportunity is still to come, with the negotiations over the five year budget perspective for the years 1993-8 in the Community just beginning. The clause from the protocol on economic and social cohesion in the Maastricht Treaty, which we quoted above, makes this clear, as it continues that the signatories

'[REAFFIRM] the need to review on the occasion [1992], the appropriate size of the [Structural] Funds in the light of the tasks of the Community in the area of economic and social cohesion'

The budgetary perspective for 1993-8

Four issues stand out in the negotiation of the new budget framework, which will impinge on cohesion: an increase in size for the structural funds; a major change in the emphasis on agriculture; an adjustment to budget shares on the grounds of equity; and an expansion of the budget as a whole.

In 1988 a commitment to double the structural funds over the five-year budget perspective was adopted. The pressure this time round is to double them again. This is not an unrealistic proposal. In NIESR (1991) we showed that if agricultural spending is held constant in real terms, the budget continues to grow at 3 per cent a year, in real terms, as it has over recent years, and all other programmes retain their share, then this alone would result in an increase in the structural funds by about one third (table 3). Adopting a harsher stance on agriculture, which might stem anyway from an agreement in the Uruguay Round, a somewhat slower increase in the share of other policies and a slightly faster rate of increase in the budget as a whole, could still enable redoubling, within the current constraint that the size of the budget should not exceed 1.4 per cent of Community GDP.

There is also the revenue side of the budget to consider. One of the reasons why the Community appears to have a rather anomalous structure of net contributions (chart 1) is that Community revenues are based on what is known as 'own resources', of which there are four at present. The first two are the customs revenues from imports from third countries and the agricultural levies. The third resource is 1 per cent of VAT receipts on a standardised basis. The first two resources depend for their incidence on the structure of trade patterns and the importance of external agricultural trade in the structure of the economy. Neither are therefore particularly related to a country's economic advantage. VAT receipts are a much better, but still imperfect, measure. It is only the fourth resource, which does not have to be called on at present, which is directly related to GDP.

Revenues are collected on a member state basis and parallel calculations on their regional incidence to that of the regional incidence of Community expenditure have not, to our knowledge, been made in any detail. Nevertheless a switch towards the third and, particularly, the fourth resource could have a major impact on the equity and regional impact of the Community's budget. In one sense this switch might apply directly, if the degree of subsidisation of agriculture falls and, hence, the second resource becomes less important. Similarly, if the budget as a whole rises in size, existing resources will tend to become inadequate and marginal revenues will come from the more equitably assessed sources. The

Commission's current proposal to raise real spending by 30 per cent over the period up to 1998 makes a substantial switch towards the fourth resource.

An alternative would be to raise a fifth own resource, which had a clearly equitable base. Discussions in the European Parliament have raised the idea of a European Tax, which would be some element of income tax in the Community, so that all citizens could feel some direct sense of involvement in the Community's activities. There is of course the risk that any new tax would attract unpopularity, even though it represents an increase in fairness and does not have any impact on the Community's overall tax burden. Using income tax is a surer way of redistributing from the richer citizens to the poorer citizens, than is a concentration purely on expenditure based taxes (although this would be less true if the expenditure tax were more broadly based). Currently the revenue implications of the Community are hidden from the individual taxpayer. The more these costs are brought out into the open the clearer the gross cost of Community is and this might lead to increased popular pressure to cut spending.

A second possibility which has been widely canvassed is the idea of a fuel or carbon tax. This in itself could be said to be European in character as airborne pollution is exported at present without any reference to the polluter pays principle. Since the new Treaty explicitly includes new provisions on the environment a change of this form might very well appear appropriate.

The imbalance in net contributions to the Community compared with GDP per head, shown in chart 1, is of the proportion that will require action from the current budgetary discussions. Not only is it really rather absurd that two of the rather better off member states, Denmark and the Netherlands, should continue to be net beneficiaries from the system, in virtue of the strength of their agriculture, but that Spain should become a net contributor this year is patently inequitable. Other more minor alterations look desirable, particularly increasing the degree to which Portugal is a net beneficiary.

To a large extent, tackling the problems posed by the system of agricultural support will itself rectify most of the anomalies. As chart 2, drawn from Franzmeyer *et al.*, 1991, shows, while the structural funds result in a substantial focus of spending on the less advantaged regions, agricultural price support does not. Since agricultural spending of this sort forms more than half of the total budget, total spending is only mildly directed towards the less favoured. In the Community of nine, agricultural price support was more effective in redistributing resources but the accession of the three new Mediterranean countries in the 1980s changed the picture as the CAP support is aimed far more at Northern rather than Southern products.

Replacement of the principle of price support by a simpler system aimed at the problems of rural communities could be dovetailed with the use of the structural funds for all types of problem areas to help improve cohesion. The latest measures for reforming the structural funds go some way down this avenue, by offering income support to farmers on small and hill holdings. The pressures on the CAP, externally through the Uruguay Round, internally from the need to have a fairer and better directed Community budget and from its own obvious inadequacy, may have some impact on this occasion. Certainly, a failure of the GATT Round will not only reduce growth and potential economic welfare but it will make the process of adjustment for convergence more difficult, as general levels of unemployment will tend to rise. It will also increase the distortions and, hence, poor allocations in the system, tending by and large to slow the pace of change rather than accelerate it, as it is existing products facing rising competition which are the usual target of new trade restraints.

Although reform of the CAP may do a lot to remove remaining budgetary worries, it is worth noting Franzmeyer et al's finding, that many other policies' expenditure programmes do not have a profile which is slanted towards the less favoured regions. The most obvious is research and technology development policy. Not surprisingly policy is slanted towards those regions in which research facilities are concentrated, which are typically advanced urban areas, with some exceptions for agricultural, environmental or hazardous products. While, of course, it would be inappropriate to insist that all policies should have any specific regional focus, it would be sensible, in formulating the expenditure programmes, to be aware of their regional impact, as otherwise such programmes may merely serve to emphasise existing disparities. As Hingel (1991) has pointed out, there are clear examples where RTD linkages, operating over new networks of widely separated regions in the Community, can open ideas which would otherwise have remained dormant with traditional links.

The appropriate structures for having an equitable budgetary system, yet one which continues to foster an efficient allocation of resources, has been thoroughly studied by Padoa-Schioppa (1987) inter alia. He suggests that a band can be set round a target relation of GDP per head to net budgetary contribution. This is illustrated in chart 3, where a logarithmic relation between the two variables is proposed. Under these circumstances, the net benefit received by low GDP per head member states rises more than proportionately and net contribution for the high GDP per head member states rises less than proportionately. This both concentrates the benefits where they are needed most and spreads the contribution more widely. Others' views of what constitutes equity will no doubt vary from this.

If the expected outturn for a particular member state lies outside the agreed bands then it would be asked to make an extra contribution or would receive a rebate to bring it back inside the bounds. Ex-post adjustment would also be possible. The particular width of the bands, which could be of fixed proportion to GDP per head or fixed, are also largely a matter of political decision. Having them narrower would increase the ex-ante and ex-post changes that need to be made. Having them wider would permit greater anomalies to persist.

Further measures

These equalisation arrangements fall short of the idea of providing direct fiscal transfers to the less favoured regions, either through the Commission or directly through a European counterpart to the länderfinanzausgleich in Germany, whereby the richer regions provide an element of transfer to the less well off. Fiscal transfers are not viewed with favour in the Community at present — except by the likely recipients that is, particularly at the local level (see House of Lords, 1992, for example, for suggestions from the UK, Italy and Spain in favour of such 'unhypothecated' transfers). The objection is based on the fact that there is no guarantee what the extra funds will be used for. As expenditure programmes exist at present, they are entirely dedicated to particular items of spending at a very detailed level. Although there are arguments about additionality — whether Community expenditure actually adds to what the member state would have done without that contribution — the Community does know, with considerable certainty, how funds have been used.

Fiscal transfers are only justified in the long run if it is felt that there are no mechanisms available which will otherwise reduce disparities. They are thus, in a sense, an admission of failure. In an ideal world, the market mechanisms within an EMU will reduce disparities. However, it is over optimistic to expect that somehow the EC would be able to reduce disparities through market mechanisms by more than large nation states like the US and Canada find they can manage. Since the EC does not have the balancing mechanisms of a tax and benefit system, it must expect that it will have to use more indirect mechanisms, like fiscal transfers, if it wants to achieve a degree of cohesion similar to that of such nation states.

An alternative route, therefore, is to expand the Community's competences to provide some of these cohesive mechanisms. We have suggested two areas in which this might occur in (NIESR, 1991). The first is to expand the sorts of project eligible under the structural funds. These could, in particular, include a wider range of social infrastructure, such as hospitals and schools and to expand the help which can be given to human capital to include a wide range of education and training for those in work as well as those out of it. The second would be to introduce a social security fund or a similar mechanism which provided a contribution to those households in difficulty in disadvantaged regions. In the spirit of the principle of subsidiarity, these funds would be transfered to the member states for spending in the regions, under the structure of their own social security systems. The only requirement would be one of additionality. Such a system increases the chance that the Community's programmes are transfering resources from the richer in the Community to the poorer. In the existing system there is a danger that there is a transfer from the poorer in rich regions to the richer in poorer regions. The emphasis on agricultural price support has a greater proportionate incidence on lower income households, for example. A focus on infrastructure projects directs payments towards the construction and equipment industries. The equipment is likely to come from outside the less favoured regions and, where specialists are required for the projects, even the labour may come from outside the region, as may the construction companies themselves.

Some of the regional difficulties relate purely to questions of transition, particularly to the changes which have to be implemented to achieve the preconditions for monetary union. A transitory problem can be dealt with by transitory solutions. Social security systems are intended to act as stabilisers during periods of difficulty and the size of their expenditure varies with the economic cycle. One widely canvassed transitory mechanism of this form (see MacDougall, 1977, for example) is to create an unemployment fund for the Community as a whole into which employees/employers contribute and from which funds can be drawn by those regions with high unemployment to stimulate employment. Objectives 3 and 4 in the current structural funds programme have this sort of aim but their scale could be expanded to ease new problems from the implementation of EMU.

Finally, one could consider whether the Community offers the full range of mechanisms of the international system in helping problems of adjustment. The structural funds and the European Investment Bank offer a mix of grants and loans for specific structural development, akin to the mix of loans and grants available from multilateral agencies, like the World Bank. The range of help available, on a basis similar to the IMF, to assist member states with transitional problems is rather more limited. Greece has been the only beneficiary in recent years and there the facility to draw further has been halted, pending the implementation of several of the fiscal changes agreed as a condition of the loans. Short-run finance is available for the smoothing operations in exchange markets but, perhaps, a wider form of IMF-style finance would be of assistance for such a transitional problem, rather than the use of outright fiscal transfers, which might not change behaviour, as they do not need to be paid back. The competence for such temporary provision lies with the EMI.

Concluding remark

The problems of real convergence have been neglected in much of the direct discussion of the preconditions for EMU, although their importance was clearly spelt out in the Delors Report. If there turns out to be a worsening of real disparities in the next few years this could prove to be a major issue when it comes to the practice of convergence during the 1990s. The Community has the opportunity, in the current negotiations over the budgetary perspective for 1993-8, to take steps to tackle this, before it threatens the successful achievement of EMU and the Commission has made this clear in presenting its initial proposals. Reform of the structural funds themselves and reform of the budget as a whole offer considerable opportunities for tackling the problems of real convergence, even without any major increase in total spending. The process enabling EMU to come into place in the 1990s is not ended by the Maastricht agreement, much of the practical action is still to come.

Table 1 *The Objectives of EC Structural Policy and their Percentage Shares, 1989-93*

Objective	Description	%
1	Lagging regions	63
2	Declining regions	12
3	Long-term unemployment)	
4	Youth unemployment)	12
5a	Agricultural adjustment	6
5b	Rural development	5
	Other	2

Table 2 *Indices of GDP/head in 1989 (EC12=100)*

Country	GDP index	Country	GDP index
Belgium	101	Ireland	64
Denmark	107	Italy	104
West Germany	112	Luxembourg	129
Greece	54	Netherlands	102
Spain	77	Portugal	55
France	109	UK	107

Source: *Eurostat Rapid Report 1991, no. 2.*

Table 3 *1992 Community Budget (draft)*

Area of spending	ecu mn.	%
EAGGF*Guarantee section	34,660	53.2
Structural operations	17,965	27.6
Policies with multiannual allocations	2,700	4.0
Other policies	5,048	7.7
Repayments and administration	3,833	5.9

Agricultural fund.

Chart 1 *Ratio of 'member states' contributions to receipts (% of the Community budget, 1989)*

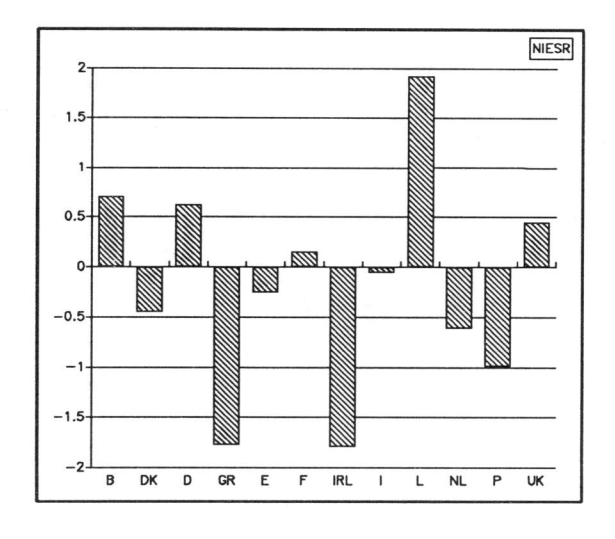

78   *Achieving Monetary Union in Europe*

Chart 2   *Regional concentration of EC payments, 1986-87, EC12*

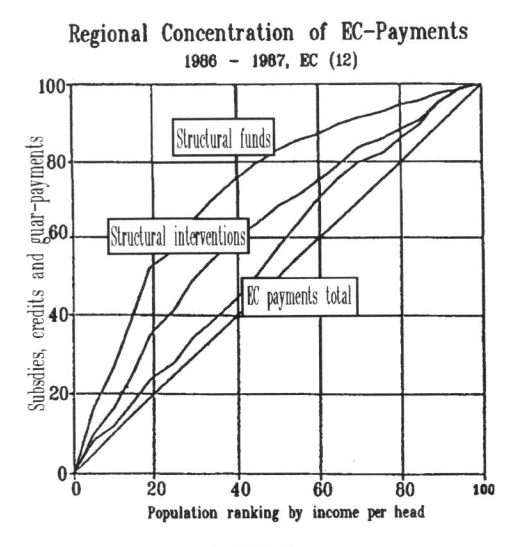

Source: Franzmeyer et al. (1991).

Chart 3   *An equity safeguard mechanism for the Community budget*

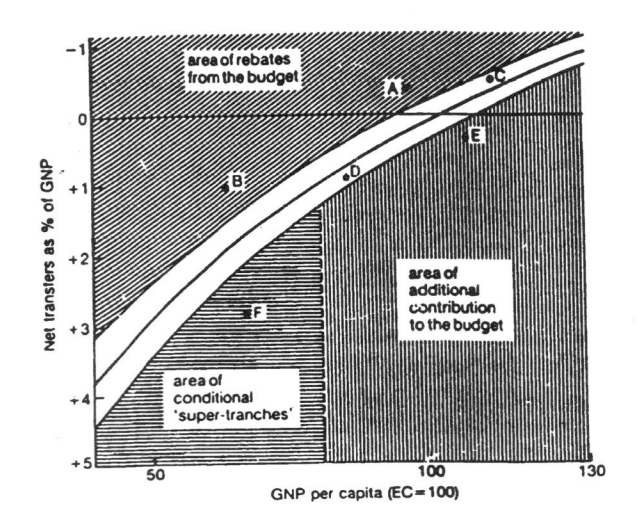

Source: Padoa-Schioppa (1987).

6

Broadening the Community

Up till even three years ago, planning for the future of the Community, even on a relatively long-term basis, was a relatively straightforward matter. Most of Europe was in one of three camps. Countries were either in the CMEA, EFTA or EC groupings. Only Turkey, Cyprus, Malta and in the long run, perhaps Yugoslavia, were unattached and potential members of the EC within a time frame worth contemplating. Albania was in a class of its own. The EFTA countries looked reasonably firmly set within their own framework, as issues of neutrality restricted all, except Norway and Iceland, from applying for membership. Their path forward from the free trade agreements seemed set for the European Economic Space, which would in effect extend most of the benefits of the single market to them. Within that framework of stability, it made a lot of sense for the Community to look inward in planning the next stage of integration and to move to full economic and monetary integration.

The changes in central and eastern Europe, with the introduction of democracy, the moves towards a market economy and the break up of the Soviet Union have transformed the picture. Six new countries have been created out of the former Soviet Union, which lie at least partly in Europe, three have been created from the break up of Yugoslavia, East Germany has joined West Germany and the process is too unstable to suggest that all the political boundary changes have now been made. It is now reasonable to assume that all these countries are potential members of a European Community, which would make a Community of 32. Sweden and Austria have already formally applied for full membership and Finland is likely to add itself to the list this year. The neat picture of a Community, proceeding through the stages of closer integration, together, now looks decidedly inappropriate. Not only are there strains for the newer member states from the increased speed of integration, which we have discussed in the last chapter and go on to consider on a country by country basis in the next, but as integration deepens, so the process of transition for a new member becomes more complex.

This does not mean that transition periods have to become longer. On the contrary, East Germany has joined the Community with a negotiation period of just a few months and a short transition period. In particular, in terms of monetary union, it has moved immediately to the core of the system, adopting the D-Mark as its currency. Sweden, Austria and Finland are also set to have a very short transition period and, probably, a short negotiation period as well. They already have free trade agreements with the EC in manufactures, they have already agreed, through the European Economic Area agreement, to adopt rules applying to the single market, and Austria in particular has a strong currency and a high level of convergence already towards meeting the preconditions for full economic and monetary union. Indeed, it is reasonable to expect them to overtake several of the existing member states in the process of integration during the next few years. They are not, of course, without problems. Sweden and Finland subsidise their agriculture even more than the EC and they have regional problems, particularly with the North. There will be considerable structural change as a consequence, for which they are already preparing.

If the other EFTA countries decided to apply and were successful, there is no reason to think that they too could not have short transition periods and that this broadening of the Community would, far from acting as a threat to EMU, actually strengthen it, because these countries could realistically hope to become full members inside the existing timetable. If they also could meet the convergence conditions by 1997 or 1999, together with most of the existing members, EMU would get off to a very good start and the ecu would immediately become a world currency to rival the dollar.

The position for the other potential members of the Community is completely different. They are all low income countries compared with the existing members. The central and eastern European countries are embarking on a process of economic transformation and are simultaneously reorganising their trading patterns from a planned arrangement among themselves to an open, market-based pattern in which Western Europe and the EC in particular will play a major role. Until the process of economic and particularly political change has stabilised, the nature of integration is likely to be fairly cautious. The degree of economic deprivation and disorder being endured in some regions at present is quite sufficient to stimulate violence or a coup. Even when this stabilisation has taken place, the real disparities are so great that the process of integration is likely to be relatively long drawn out.

However, it is not clear that the appropriate way to handle this period of integration is to proceed by a series of bilateral agreements that take these countries through a period of trading preferences, followed by a full free trade agreement and then progressive adoption of the rules of the single market, ending up with EMU at some time, well into the next century. Monetary stability is an early requirement of successful recovery.

Monetary and exchange-rate linkages need to be high on the agenda, not towards the end of the process. Indeed it might very well be that the ecu has a more important role to play in the next few years in Eastern Europe than it does in the existing EC, which has strong and stable currencies already. In this chapter, therefore, we explore the way that these dramatic changes in Europe and the broadening of the Community in particular impinge on the nature of EMU and the process of its achievement. There is no particular reason why the objectives of broadening the Community and proceeding to EMU for those who meet the convergence conditions should conflict. Indeed they might be complementary, with member states following various speeds of integration. The negotiations leading up to the Maastricht agreement appear to have followed a very compartmentalised approach, leaving on one side the simultaneous discussions with the former CMEA countries and their successors and the questions of the widening to include the EFTA countries. We try to reintegrate the discussion, dealing first with EFTA and then moving on to the 'southern' group of potential members, before ending up with the thorny problem of central and eastern Europe.

EFTA and monetary union

Among the EFTA countries, we face the irony that several of them are more prepared for EMU, in the sense of meeting the preconditions laid down in the Maastricht agreement, than are most of the existing member states (see table 1). Austria, for example, appears to meet all the convergence criteria already. Having them join the Community is thus, in many respects, a help rather than a complication. Adding two or three more member states will raise some bureaucratic difficulties, including the need to bring the new nationalities into Community institutions, and increasing the number of views that have to be taken into account in any discussions.

However, adding Austria, Sweden and Finland only increases the EC population by 7 per cent to 345 million and GDP by 9 per cent. The net effect is therefore reasonably small, particularly since these countries have been becoming increasingly like members of the EC without voting rights. Their trade patterns are already highly EC orientated, with (table 2) larger proportions of trade involving the EC (especially if we include their mutual trade) than for the UK, for example. As small countries, they are already heavily trade orientated (table 2) and, hence, are well integrated with the rest of the EC economy, even before membership. This integration includes not just trade but the ownership and siting of production. Swedish companies in particular, as Sweden has a disproportionately large number of major international companies for its economic size, are already participating throughout the single market. If the scope of the Community were to include Switzerland, then this pattern would be further reinforced.

The economic and social changes involved in an expansion to include Austria, Finland and Sweden are, therefore, not enormous. Sweden and Finland would increase the geographical spread of the Community considerably and, in doing so, add to the problems of peripherality. This 'northern' expansion of the Community would also tend to reinforce the disparities between the majority and the 'southern' member states, both in terms of income per head and in product structure. This is not necessarily a problem in itself, as the potential new members have already shown themselves willing to assume the burdens of structural policy, through the creation of a 1bn ecu cohesion fund, as part of the European Economic Area agreement. A further consequence of their relative wealth is that they will make a disproportionate contribution to the EC's resources, thereby either being able to reduce the general burden or increase the ability to undertake Community-wide policies, without having to make any further demands on the existing member states.

The effects on decision making are also relatively limited. The determination of qualified majorities will be affected, making it slightly easier to outvote larger countries. However, by the same token, adding three smaller countries means, more clearly than before, that a majority of the Community live in a minority of the member states. Hence, on a population or GDP basis, a majority could want something that most member states do not. In particular, the 'southern' constituency could find itself outvoted. Where unanimity is required, complexity is clearly increased.

Given the pace of change in adoption of EMU, it is clearly advantageous to get the new potential members involved from the inside at the outset. They need to participate in the process of planning and of increasing coordination of economic policies. It would help if they could enter Stage 2 from the beginning, as that stage is only planned to last from between three and five years. A major learning process is involved and full participation would enhance that, particularly in areas like central bank cooperation.

There is uncertainty over the remaining EFTA countries. Will they decide, fairly rapidly, that they wish to become full members, will they remain undecided or will it become clear that they intend to remain outside? The firm decision to remain outside is probably the easiest to handle but indecision involves establishing a structure of the Community, which could readily be adapted, should they change their minds (and should the Community wish to admit them). Expanding the Community beyond fifteen to up to nineteen does start to pose much more major problems of organisation. The Commision currently has seventeen members but it is thought likely that the current review will recommend a reduction in that number and a reduction in the number of directorates general, so that policy can be more coordinated and efficiently applied.

Expanding the number of countries substantially could start to introduce tensions between the numbers of officials and representatives needed for efficiency and those needed for political reasons. It is likely to expand the size of the governing council of the ECB. There the need to form an inner executive, on which there will not be members from several member states, has already been recognised. This process will need to be extended still further to other parts of the administration of the Community if they are to remain effective, otherwise there is a danger of the system collapsing under its own weight. The more member states, the more official languages, although this is not the case for Austria, Switzerland and Liechtenstein. Each of these complications makes it harder to run the Community and stresses the need for an improvement in its efficiency.

The most important case for monetary union occurs with several of the EFTA countries still not being full members. The question arises, could they become part of a monetary union, without full membership? In technical terms, given the high degree of their integration and the European Economic Area agreement, the answer would be yes, if they accepted the controls on their fiscal policy. It is a different question, however, whether either they or the Community would want such an arrangement. What is more likely is that they might wish to lock their currencies to the ecu, possibly changing the denomination so that they hold one-to-one parity. It would even be possible for them to allow the ecu to be legal tender, thereby simplifying the process of transactions between themselves and the Community and increasing the degree of integration. Clearly it is always open to them to try to run their fiscal and monetary policies consistent with those of the EC, so that parity is maintained. Indeed, they can, if they wish, take outside advice on how that policy should be followed.

However, even if accorded some form of observer status within some of the relevant Community policymaking bodies, they would always be followers rather than contributing to the policy setting directly. The major problem would come with maintaining parities in the foreign exchange market, as the EC central banks are much bigger players in the market and could always dominate the actions of the EFTA central banks, if they wished. If very narrow margins are to be maintained credibly then some sort of cooperative arrangement is required among the central banks, even if it only involves the EC banks (ECB after EMU) in an orderly marketing agreement.

There is some temptation to retain an external facet of the ecu system, as the settlement mechanism is currently run by the Bank for International Settlements in Basle and the secretariat for the Committee of EC Central Banks is also run from there. The crucial step will be the siting of the European Monetary Institute. It has the potential to take on the role for the integration of the wider European system and not just the current EC members. A growing out of the BIS framework might make a lot of sense but the timing of any Swiss participation does not seem to make this likely and a new institution, inside the existing Community and not so concerned with the wider role, seems likely. This is another instance of the importance of timing.

If changes involving EFTA countries are to have effect from the inception of Stage 2, they have to occur quickly. As we have already indicated, this swift action will have a number of benefits for EMU and increase its chances of successful implementation. It does, however, pose a problem for those potential applicants from among the EFTA countries, who have not yet made up their minds. The decision-making process in Switzerland is inherently slow, not just because of the difficulty of making such a major change away from neutrality and non-involvement in 'political' international organisations. The role of the cantons and the need for a 'popular' decision by the voting population makes any rapid moves unlikely. Even though membership by Austria would leave Switzerland enclosed by the EC a slow decision-making process would give the opportunity for a working equilibrium with Switzerland outside EMU to be established and, hence, decrease the likelihood of the change. Alternatively, it might prove very difficult to establish such an equilibrium, increasing the pressure on Switzerland to change but this is much less likely.

Liechtenstein is likely to follow Switzerland but Norway is in a rather different position, having successfully negotiated membership of the EC along with the UK, Denmark and the Irish Republic in 1972, only to have it narrowly rejected in a referendum. This narrow balance has continued over the intervening years. With Finland and Sweden opting to join and Denmark already in, the balance may very well tip in favour of membership again. Norway, with a heavier weight from oil, maritime, forestry and other resources in its economy is a little less structurally convergent than some of the other EFTA countries but this is unlikely to be to the extent that membership of EMU would impose any greater strains than it does on some of the exisiting member states. It would seem likely, therefore, that Norway will choose to participate at some stage but it is particularly likely to try to arrange a close association with the new monetary system, as it is already shadowing the ERM of the EMS successfully, as is Sweden. Iceland's geographical separation makes it a special case.

Taken together, therefore, the increasing pace of change inside the Community may be encouraging other countries to wish to join, particularly in EFTA. The further step of full EMU is not a disincentive; indeed there are arguments for speeding up the accession process for the current applicants. Expanding the EC to include the whole of EFTA would entail an important reorganisation of the administration of the Community but it does not imply that the form or timetable of the Maastricht Treaty require amendment. Broadening the EC and deepening to achieve EMU do not appear contradictory.

A southwards expansion?

Expanding the EC in other directions in Europe presents much greater problems and might very well require a different sort of structure, towards which an EMU where only some of the member states move to Stage 3 of EMU at the outset may actually provide some pointers. The time frame for full integration is, however, very different from that we have been discussing for EFTA.

Turkey has been keen to join the EC for twenty years and has had its application on the table over this period. There seems very little likelihood that the position will change. Turkey has been steadily integrating with the Community during its period of Association and 53 per cent of its exports went to the EC in 1990. It has a very low income per head, which is only 13 per cent of the EC average. This is acting as a considerable advantage from the point of view of inward investment. EC companies are setting up factories, particularly in industries such as clothing, textiles and footwear, and reimporting inside the tariff barrier, because of Turkey's associate status. Other industries where labour costs are important and the acquisition of production skills is straightforward, in areas such as light engineering, are also developing because management, product development and marketing skills can all be brought in from the EC. German firms have been particularly active, aided in part by the fact that several German managers have become fluent in Turkish and familiar in dealing with Turkey as a result of the large Turkish contingent of *Gastarbeiter*. It remains to be seen how much their focus is being changed by the new opportunities in the Eastern Länder.

Although the economics of possible membership may be slowly improving, the politics are unchanged. Admission of new members requires unanimity and Greece is opposed to such entry, irrelevant of any argument about whether Turkey is really a European country. The other problem with Turkey is its sheer size. It has a population of 51 million, which would make it one of the largest member states. Accommodating a small member state with a very low income per head might be possible, under the terms of the EC's structural policy, but the membership of a large and much poorer country, like Turkey, would turn it upside down. To accommodate such countries a new approach would be needed. However, given the problems in central/eastern Europe, such a mechanism might be forthcoming, from which Turkey could benefit. Turkey is playing a large and largely unreported practical role in opening up the Russian market and the market in the neighbouring former soviet states near Turkey's northeastern border.

The two (three) remaining southern potential members are Malta and Cyprus. Since these are small states, they could easily be accommodated by the EC but they are also lower income than most of the existing member states. Cyprus also has the problem of division and there is considerable reluctance to get involved with these difficulties. There is thus little chance that much will happen in the way of a further southern expansion of the Community. The dramatic developments in the CMEA and the wish by the EC to take action there make activity further south even less likely in the short run, except in so far as the shape of Europe might change, with a wider range of forms of linkage to the EC or a secondary grouping.

Eastern and central Europe, a major problem and an opportunity for the ecu

The rapid redrawing of the map of Europe makes it difficult to decide how to delimit the discussion of the issues posed by the possible path of wider integration for the Maastricht Treaty. There have been several discussions of the redrawing of appropriate boundaries (Wallace, 1991, for example) based not just on economic criteria but on culture, religion and traditional linkages. Initial attention has been directed towards the EC's immediate neighbours, which formed part of the western European system before the war. Although boundaries may have been redrawn these countries existed as separate entities on the international scene. Now the break up of the Soviet Union has taken place this may add the Baltic States to the list of more immediate neighbours with whom links will be developed relatively rapidly, perhaps on a traditional Baltic basis. The Community is already extending the links it initially developed with Poland, Hungary and Czechoslovakia to Romania and Bulgaria and its involvement in peacekeeping in Yugoslavia shows its commitment there. How far the discussion can extend to the members of the Commonwealth of Independent States, which lie wholly or partly within Europe, is much more speculative.

Economic and political linkages with all these countries are bound to develop, provided the democratisation process continues. The mechanisms of linkage, through trade, investment, joint ventures of various forms, lending, financial aid, technical assistance and food and other aid pose a range of problems. Some of these are related directly to the process of European union, in particular the role of the ecu in both payments between east and west and indeed within the east itself.

Behaviour in Western Europe regarding the transformation of Central and Eastern Europe has been understandably tentative. Both public and private sectors have been relatively reluctant to commit funds to projects until the way forward is clearer. Not only has the political outlook appeared somewhat dubious but the economic viability of many enterprises has proved to be very shaky on closer examination. The experience in the former East Germany has been most instructive. Initially, it had been thought that it would prove possible to transform a large proportion of existing enterprises by an appropriate injection of capital from West Germany and other western countries. In part, this view was based on the idea that change could be relatively gradual, improving quality and, hence, developing existing markets further east, while exploiting lower costs to develop markets in the west, often as part of the product range of existing western companies.

In practice, the market further east has collapsed. On closer examination, existing firms have been shown to require investment on such a scale that many have not been viable. Some of this reflects not just the technology used but the degree of pollution from some of the plants. The result has been a collapse in output and consequent major unemployment. West German employers have also been rather disappointed to find that what was supposed to be the best qualified workforce in Eastern Europe has turned out to have poor motivation and lack of suitable skills for modern production methods. As a result, not only has consumption switched very strongly towards western goods but, despite capacity restraints, many West German producers have chosen to supply the east by expansion of production in the west. There have also been problems of property rights. It has not been clear to the inward investor who the owner of the assets might be, the current operators, the former owners, a government holding board or some prospective, more disaggregated, form of shareholding. Until these issues are sorted out, investors are not surprisingly hesitant.

The other eastern countries present different degrees of similar problems but they also share the problem of price adjustment from a system where not only have prices been distorted from their world market levels but, as a consequence, quantities available, let alone quality, are well away from the likely equilibrium. In some countries, like Poland, hyperinflation has resulted and one of the major needs has been to stabilise the currency. In the Soviet Union, not only had the government been printing money at a rapid rate to cover the huge deficit but, because of the lack of goods in the shops and controlled prices, people had built up considerable cash balances. The opportunities for major inflation and collapse of the currency are therefore considerable in a number of these states.

The most suitable forms of assistance from the EC in these circumstances are, therefore, not straightforward. Clearly the traditional remedies of openness to trade and inward investment will be important but, given the problems of producing competitive products in the short run, opening the EC more widely to agricultural products may make considerable sense. Direct assistance has taken the form of emergency aid and technical assistance, concentrating first of all on Poland, Hungary and Czechoslovakia, then extending to the other Eastern European countries and to the components of the former Soviet Union. With more comprehensive assistance, including that from the European Bank for Reconstruction and Development, the EC has an opportunity to do more to help stabilise the currencies of Eastern Europe and to assist the structure of payments through a wider role for the ecu.

Not only is the ecu likely to be the main instrument for lending but it reflects more closely the sorts of trading patterns these countries are likely to have. Fixing exchange rates at this stage is clearly unreasonable but having a steady slowdown through a crawling peg against the ecu might very well be helpful. Stabilising the currency will also permit at least partial convertibility, which in turn will assist the encouragement of inward investment. If the ecu does not fulfil this role other currencies will be used. The principal candidates are the US dollar and particularly the D-Mark. Both of these lack attraction in the context of increasing European integration. The former involves an external link which could be unstable because economic linkages are not likely to be dollar dominated and hence there will be a mismatch in price movements. The latter is likely to be much more successful but is a step away from the progress to the single currency rather than towards it.

The problem which countries face in these circumstances is that the process of adjustment is extremely painful, involving major falls in GDP as a whole and reductions in real wages for individuals. This does not win governments brownie points with their electorates and there is an enormous temptation to ease the attempt to stabilise the currency and increase the deficit in order to remain in power. Such easings usually result in a loss of credibility and a collapse in the programme, thereby wasting much of the hardship. The experience of Latin American countries is very much one of failed attempts rather than sustained successes. Collignon (1992) inter alia has suggested that a clear programme of closer association with the EC as 'convergence' proceeds will help both the success of stabilisation and its credibility. A closer involvement of the EC, where assistance is linked to the achievement of agreed targets, would give both traders and investors an extra degree of certainty in what is clearly a high risk circumstance.

Appeal is often made to the example of postwar recovery in western Europe, with the role of Marshall aid and the easing of the hard currency shortages through the European Payments Union. In such circumstances the achievement of successful recovery becomes far more of a multilateral responsibility than a series of bilateral agreements. Collignon suggests extending the ideas behind the EMU stages and having a surveillance board composed of representatives from the East European countries themselves, the EMI, IMF, BIS and EBRD. The member countries would subscribe a proportion of their reserves to the common pool. The EC would provide short-term standby support for the currency pool. Longer-term finance would presumably be a mixture of IMF and EC funds administered very much along traditional IMF lines.

The relevant question here is whether the East European countries will wish to cooperate with each other rather than just with the EC. There is an obvious incentive for the most successful eastern countries to try to become part of a favoured inner circle, as appeared to be the case with the initial programmes, aimed only at Poland, Hungary and Czechoslovakia. Clearly at some stage some countries will be ready for each opportunity for closer integration, should they wish it, before others. Indeed, given the enormous variety in Eastern Europe, any plan which has credibility must treat them individually and flexibly.

Poland, Hungary and Czechoslovakia may be most ready, followed by Bulgaria and and lastly Romania, all of which have at least existed as separate countries since the war. The three Baltic states, although independent before the war, have to re-establish their identity and structures, while the Ukraine, Byelorussia and the Russian Federation have over seven decades within the communist system. No-one of working age has experience of a market economy and deliberate integration to reduce national identities means that they are starting from a point even further from the market. Until recently, Yugoslavia would have been considered the most market-orientated of the countries to the east of the Community. However, until the fighting stops it is right off the agenda and even afterwards it will require a careful assessment before it is possible to decide on the extent of the damage and the readiness of the various parts to move forward.

The argument is extended beyond the simple international transactions and macroeconomic policy prescriptions to suggesting that where new rules are introduced for regulating the market, they should model themselves on their EC equivalents. This would make the transition easier when the markets ultimately come together - assuming of course that this was in fact the aim of the East European countries. The EC would thus play a major role in the recovery of the rest of Europe and in some respects the ecu would play a more important role outside the EC in the early stages of adjustment before the EC itself adopts it as its single currency in Stage 3.

Broadening and deepening

The major worry expressed has been that expanding the Community would imperil the progress to EMU. It has been thought that having more members would complicate the process of getting agreement and delay implementation of the various stages. In practice this now seems unlikely. Most of the single market legislation has now been agreed and the process for reaching EMU has now been set out at Maastricht. What we have shown in this chapter is that the expansion of the Community, in the short run, to include Austria, Finland and Sweden, is likely to assist rather than hinder the process of integration, because of the net contribution they will make to the budget and the degree to which they have already converged. Expanding much further, however, will put additional pressure on the current mechanisms of the Community. It would, in any case, be wise, in the current reforms of the Commission structure, to look forward to that wider Community and plan accordingly. Such more efficient structures are needed for the running of an EMU, not an organisation which grows ever heavier with time.

Extensions beyond the EFTA countries do not look possible in the next few years. They would involve countries with GDP per head well below those of the existing member states and would lead to strains on the structural policy, which already may be inadequate to achieve the necessary real convergence and cohesion for the least favoured regions of the Community. Less demanding methods will, therefore, have to be used to assist other non-member European countries. It seems inevitable, given the sheer scale of the needs of the Eastern European countries and the opportunities they offer as new markets as they become more open, that some of the funds attracted from both public and private sectors will substitute for spending elsewhere in the Community. Where those funds relate to the attraction of inward investment, it may act to the disadvantage of the less favoured regions. The increased emphasis on investment will also tend to drive up interest rates, which may also have adverse transition consequences for those countries hoping to reduce their interest rate burden.

Finally, there is a tendency to forget the impact of the EC's activities on the rest of the world, by concentrating on both the internal benefits of EMU and the problems of its immediate neighbours to the east. In trying to deal with the problems of Eastern Europe and take a leading role in the EBRD, the EC is trying to play a world role, acting on behalf of others because it is best placed to do so. The fact, therefore, that some of these changes have an adverse effect elsewhere, on competing agricultural producers, for example, is, in a sense, their share of the total cost. In the case of EMU, however, the intention is less benign.

Much of the point of EMU is to improve efficiency within the EC and to improve competitiveness. Hence the relative position of the EC is intended to improve. In dealing with outside countries the EC has tried to convince them that the process of EMU will be of worldwide benefit by increasing the growth of Europe and hence its demand for imports and overseas investment which will help the gains spill over. The European market is also becoming increasingly open for others to participate in the gains. The detail of the benefits can be questioned (see Mayes et al., 1992) and it is clear that certain aspects of integration cause serious disquiet, principally the CAP and aspects of commercial policy, including antidumping. What is notable, however, is that there has been no obvious objection to monetary union. This move to increasing exchange rate and price stability in Europe seems to attract general approval, even though it may reduce the importance of the dollar in international transactions, because it will help improve monetary stability in the world as a whole. This particular step towards union in Europe will create the largest single currency area in the world in value terms. It represents the sort of step towards a role for Europe as a whole that the founders of the Community had in mind at its inception.

Table 1 *Convergence indicators of EFTA countries, 1990*

	Current balance % of GDP	Unemployment % rate	Consumer price index annual % change	General government financial balance % of GDP	Gross public debt as % of GDP
Austria	0.5	3.3	3.2	1.1	55
Finland	-4.9	3.5	5.8	1.4	15
Norway	3.4	5.2	4.5	2.3	42
Sweden	-2.6	1.5	9.3	3.9	45
Switzerland	3.8	0.6	5.4	..	..

Source: OECD.

Table 2 *Openness and integration of EFTA with EC*

	Share of exports going to EC (%)	Share of exports in GDP (%)
Austria	76	40
Finland	47	25
Norway	65	41
Sweden	54	32
Switzerland	57	38

Source: OECD

7

The Member States

Economic and monetary union will not proceed unless and until a sufficient number of the member states of the Community are considered ready to participate. Readiness is defined rather precisely in terms of the convergence criteria according to which the economic performance of each state will be judged when the time comes to move to the third stage of EMU.

Simulations using the NIESR Global Econometric Model (Anderton, *et al.*, 1992) suggest that achieving the conditions for convergence in inflation (Chart 1) and budget deficits (Chart 2) is indeed possible by 1997-9 with little problem in terms of the current balance (Chart 3) for the four major EC economies, although unemployment in France and Italy remains at a high level (Chart 4). But, when that time comes, these arithmetical calculations may not be the only, or the decisive, consideration. So far as Britain and Denmark are concerned an expression of willingness to join is also necessary; the other member states are in principle committed to join if they are able to do so, but in practice the attitude of governments and public opinion at the time will be of importance as well. The convergence criteria may be interpreted more generously for a member state which is close to the borderline and enthusiastic about joining, than it would be if opinion in the country itself was wavering. Despite the treaty commitment it is hard to imagine a member state being obliged to join if it did not wish to. It would not be difficult after all for the government of that state to make sure it failed at least one criterion, for example by devaluing its exchange rate.

In this chapter, therefore, although we shall be concerned mainly with the progress of each member state towards economic convergence, it will be appropriate also to consider in some cases the attitudes of governments and peoples to European integration and to the form in which EMU is to be introduced. It is appropriate also to say a little about the structure and institutions of some member states, since the success of the whole EMU enterprise will depend on those being compatible. It will become clear in the course of the chapter that some member states will need to undergo much more fundamental change than others. Some have already introduced major institutional reforms which will facilitate their eventual participation in EMU. One purpose of this chapter is to assess, for each country in turn, what more needs to be done. Their progress towards convergence so far can be judged from the set of tables and charts 5-7 at the end of this chapter. For further discussion see Anderton, Barrell and in't Veld (1992) and also Anderton, Barrell and McHugh (1992).

Germany

In terms of population, and of total output, the German economy was the largest in Europe even before unification. The performance of the German economy has been good in comparison with many other member states over most of the postwar period judged by the usual indications of growth and inflation, internal and external balance. One reason for the popularity of EMU throughout Europe is the ambition of other member states to copy the institutions of Germany and hence, it is hoped, to share its price stability and also its prosperity.

It would seem, then, that the need for structural or institutional change would be less in Germany than in most of the other countries we shall be considering. The German economy itself will obviously be influenced by changes in the behaviour and performance of other member states and by the harmonisation of economic policy. And, of course, the German economy is now going through a major upheaval of its own as the Länder of the east are transformed and absorbed into the market system. That process will take many years to complete and must proceed in parallel with the adaptation of the German economy to EMU.

Over the last twenty years inflation in Germany has averaged 3.9 per cent a year, compared with a rate of 8.2 per cent for the European Community as a whole. In the early 1970s the rate of inflation was allowed to rise significantly in Germany, although not to anything like the same extent as in many other countries of Europe. In 1974 it was a little over 7 per cent. At the beginning of the 1980s it again rose to about 6 per cent, but it fell back sharply in the mid-1980s, and was actually negative in 1986. The experience of the early 1990s is perhaps untypical, as inflation has risen rather more in Germany than in some other European countries (with consumer prices expected to rise about 4 per cent this year in what was West Germany) but this has been attributed to the special circumstances of unification.

It is worth remarking in this context, nevertheless, that the relatively good inflation record of Germany in the 1970s and 1980s was possible only because of the appreciation of the D-Mark against other European currencies. Were it not for the prospect of a transition to EMU, and the consequent reluctance to change exchange rates in Europe, the D-Mark might well have appreciated in response to unification and to the prospect of higher interest rates as a result. If that had happened then inflation in Germany now would have been a little lower. Thus the untypical behaviour of inflation in Germany at the present time is not altogether unconnected with the prospect of transition to EMU. The circumstances are exceptional, and the effect is small, but the incident is a pointer to the anxieties which EMU could create in Germany.

The Treaty criterion on inflation is expressed in relative terms, so it would seem that there would be nothing to prevent EMU going ahead even though the goal of price stability was not being achieved. Despite that omission however the German government and the Bundesbank would be unlikely to support a move to set up EMU at all unless the rate of inflation in (West) Germany is brought down and kept very low for several successive years. (For a discussion of EMU from a German perspective see Langfeldt, 1992.)

The success of the German authorities in curbing inflation in the mid-1980s is not unconnected with the considerable rise in unemployment which took place at that time. The peak level reached a little over 7 per cent. One of the more encouraging developments of recent years is the fall in (West) German unemployment rates to under 5 per cent, although that is still higher than the rates which were typical of the 1970s or earlier decades. The experience is encouraging because it suggests that inflation can be kept in check without the need for a large and permanent rise in unemployment. Certainly there are many countries in Europe which would be happy to emulate the unemployment experience of (West) Germany in the 1980s almost as much as its inflation experience.

Statistical investigation of the relationship between the growth of wages and unemployment levels in Germany suggests that there has been no great change over the last twenty years. The indexation of wages is actually illegal and the process of wage bargaining is relatively centralised. It seems that wage growth responds to the cycle in the national economy and to the rise or fall in national unemployment, and much less and more slowly to the increase in prices. This pattern of behaviour may well reflect the experience of recent decades and public confidence in the resolve and ability of the Bundesbank to prevent inflation from accelerating. It contrasts with the labour market experience of most other member states where wages respond all too rapidly to prices, setting off an inflationary spiral, and where unemployment has to rise very steeply before the pressure for higher wages is reduced.

If EMU were an immediate prospect today Germany itself might be excluded by a strict interpretation of the criterion for the budget deficit. This too is a consequence of unification, especially the cost of transfers and subsidies in support of living standards in the eastern Länder. Typically (West) Germany has had a small deficit on the combined financial balance of central and local governments. In the recession of the mid-1970s that deficit rose as high as 5 per cent of national income, larger in those terms than the corresponding deficit at that time in France or even in the United Kingdom. A similar pattern is to be seen in the recession of the early 1980s when the deficit in Germany again went over the 'ceiling' of 3 per cent of national income now embodied in the Maastricht Treaty. Again that deficit was rather larger than the corresponding figures for France and the United Kingdom.

Thus the convergence criterion for fiscal policy could be interpreted as requiring a stricter fiscal discipline in Germany than has been observed in the past. An alternative, and perhaps better, interpretation would be that deficits in excess of 3 per cent are not excessive if they result from a cyclical downturn in the economy. This interpretation would fit well with the institutional structure of Germany where the local authorities are relatively independent, which makes the 'fine tuning' of the budget balance very difficult — and where the responsibility for price stability rests securely with the central bank.

The current level of interest rates in Germany, about 9 per cent for short-term rates compared to 4 per cent in the United States, is the cause for some concern. Convergence requires similar rates of interest throughout Europe and the market will make sure this comes about if no further realignments are expected. Thus the tight monetary policy necessary in Germany to combat inflation is transmitted to other European countries, some of them currently more worried by recession than by inflation. There is little comfort for those countries in the forecast of future, short-term interest rates implied by the market for long-term debt. Bond yield comparisons suggest that interest rates in America are expected to rise, much more than German rates are expected to fall. If this is a correct forecast, EMU is likely to take place in an environment of high real interest rates worldwide.

If the eastern Länder of Germany were a separate country applying for membership of the European institutions, that country would not be thought ready for some years to join the Community, let alone to participate in EMU. Politics rather than economics makes it possible and necessary for the old East Germany to move much faster than say Poland, Hungary and Czechoslovakia. The adaptation required for the eastern länder of Germany to prosper within an EMU is at least as great as would be required for any of the existing member states of the Community. The eastern länder have been given a number of derogations to ease their entry into the Community. And of course the convergence criteria for EMU do not apply to regions.

The population of the eastern Länder is about 16 million, compared with about 64 million in the west, so the two populations are in the ratio of one to four. Participation rates are higher in the east, but productivity levels much lower. In considering the performance of the German economy as a whole in the future, developments in the east will have a considerable weight. As yet it is difficult to measure such variables as inflation or output on a national basis, but by the time that EMU is expected the process of assimilation should be much more advanced.

The initial effect of unification was to raise the price level and to reduce output in the east very substantially. (For a description of the German monetary union and its implications see Friedman, 1992.) The increase in prices was mainly a once-for-all effect due to cuts in subsidies, especially on housing, but as the transition to a market economy continues further prices rises are to be expected. Wage levels in the east remain well below those in the west, and many are being raised despite the wide gap between productivity levels. It remains to be seen when this continuing process can be made consistent with price stability for Germany as a whole. It is clear already that unemployment, and under-employment, in the east will remain a severe social problem for Germany for a long time to come. That in turn may have its effect on German attitudes to economic policy, and to the process of closer integration of the European economy as a whole.

Obviously EMU as now intended is impossible without German participation, and, as things now stand, that participation seems assured. What is more in doubt is the attitude that the German government will take to the timetable and the initial membership of EMU. If price stability is not achieved in Germany itself then German opinion may favour delay and the exclusion of any member states on the borderline of convergence. If the assimilation of the eastern Länder proves difficult, then German opinion may opt for a narrow version of EMU so as to limit competition with its own 'developing economy'. But as a matter of arithmetic if the German inflation performance is relatively poor it will be that much easier for other member states to match it.

France

French weariness with the round of inflation, leading to exchange rate depreciation and further inflation, provided perhaps the most important motive for setting up the European Monetary System. The failure of the 'dash for growth' in the early 1980s confirmed support for the EMS as the best hope of an effective counter-inflation policy. But the wish of the French government, naturally enough, is to participate in the decisions which shape the monetary policy of Europe, not just to follow the German lead. Hence the French concern to push ahead from EMS to EMU. (For a French perspective on EMU see Bordes and Girardin, 1992.)

In the late 1960s when plans were first drawn up for monetary union, opinion was divided between the 'monetarists', often French, and the 'economists', often German. The 'monetarist' position was that fixing exchange rates would result in convergence of economic performance. The events of the 1980s can be seen as vindicating that view. The 'economists' position was that convergence should come first — a view which has been given great weight in the drafting of the Maastricht Treaty. The 'monetarist' position is still reflected in the French (and Commission) view that the transition to monetary union should come sooner rather than later, and in their strong opposition to any suggestion of a realignment in the meantime.

Although the French rate of inflation is now marginally below the German, this is a most unusual situation. Over the past twenty years inflation in France has averaged 8.1 per cent a year, closely in line with the average for the EC as a whole. The highest annual rise was in 1974 when the rate was just under 15 per cent, and the next peak in 1980 was only a little lower at over 13 per cent. Since the mid-1980s however the rate has been very constant at about 3 per cent a year.

Unemployment in France began to rise significantly in the late 1970s and continued on a rising trend until 1987 when it was over 10 per cent. Since then it has not changed greatly, and it is now about 9 per cent — substantially higher than in (West) Germany. This has to be seen as a cost which has been paid as part of the disinflation process. Labour market studies suggest that wages in France adjust rather slowly to the pressure of demand for labour, so that unemployment needs to rise to a high level for a long time before a lower rate of wage settlement can be established as the norm. A variety of measures have been introduced in recent years with the intention of making the French labour market more flexible — bargaining is now less centralised (reducing the effects of price indexation) and security of employment has been curtailed — but there is no clear evidence that the attainable combination of inflation and unemployment has been improved as a result. Some commentators blame the statutory minimum wage (the SMIC) but the extent of its influence on the average wage level is disputed.

In the early years of the EMS the French franc was devalued relative to the D-Mark on several occasions (in October 1981, June 1982, March 1983, April 1986 and January 1987) but the intervals between the moves became longer and their size became smaller. This has been called the transition from the 'soft' EMS to the 'hard' EMS, the latter being in effect a fixed-rate system. The increased 'credibility' of the fixed exchange rates have been reflected in the narrowing of interest-rate differentials between France and Germany, which for short-term rates have now almost disappeared. It seems that the inflationary spiral in France has been halted.

If this remains true, France should have no difficulty in meeting the convergence criteria of the Maastricht Treaty. French fiscal policy has been conservative and prudent for many years. The only period in recent history when the government financial deficit rose significantly was in the early 1980s during the 'dash for growth'; and even then it only reached 3.2 per cent of national income.

Those reassuring figures should not conceal the fact that the French economy has been going through major structural changes in recent years, changes which are far from complete. Whilst the German Federal Republic was committed to the market system and generally liberal trade policies from the start, France operated a system of planning and direct controls, with notable success in the 1950s and 1960s. That tradition remains, questioning each stage of decentralisation and deregulation. As an alternative pattern for economic policy it could reassert itself, if the present pattern failed to deliver stability or prosperity.

According to this alternative tradition inflation is controlled by quantitative restrictions on credit expansion in the banking system, which are easily imposed by a central bank under the direction of the government on commercial banks which are part-owned by the state. If credit control fails, price control is there in reserve. The exchange rate is fixed by intervention in the foreign exchange markets and by controls on international financial transactions. The necessary apparatus of control in France has been progressively dismantled, but the memory of its use is still very recent. The Bank of France is still not independent of government, although it is well understood that this step must be taken soon.

A rather fundamental question arises therefore about the extent to which the structure of the French economy needs to change further in order to make an EMU not just possible but also successful. It is not just an issue of the minimum degree of convergence required to set up EMU; it is more to do with the way in which the different member states will respond to the shocks which will inevitably hit the European economy from time to time after EMU is in place.

The attempt to fix exchange rates and progress towards EMU in the 1970s failed in January 1974 when the French had to drop out of the 'snake' - the band which was supposed to limit currency fluctuations. In that year inflation rose in both France and Germany in response to the shocks of commodity and oil price rises; but in Germany it rose from 6 to 7 per cent and in France from 7 to nearly 15 per cent. (In Germany the rise in output came to a halt, whilst in France it continued for another year.) This historical episode illustrates how quickly inflation rates can diverge if economies respond very differently to a common shock. At that time, now nearly two decades ago, the French and German economies were more different than they are now. The degree of political commitment in both countries to European unity is much greater now as well. History serves as a warning, although it never repeats itself exactly.

Shocks of the magnitude experienced in 1972-4 are fortunately rather rare events. It is more likely than not that the rates of inflation in France and Germany will continue for the next few years much in line with one another, and that the exchange rate between the French franc and the D-Mark will remain largely unquestioned.

If only France and Germany were involved, EMU could begin very soon, subject of course to the independence of the Bank of France. Equally it is unlikely that EMU will ever take place at all unless France is able to participate. But the French in particular would prefer EMU to begin with at least all the larger member states involved from the start — and for that they may have to wait.

Italy

The participation of Italy in EMU from the start is still uncertain. Clearly the Italian government and the Bank of Italy are keen to join. Undoubtedly, taking a longer-term view, the Italian economy has moved a long way towards convergence with France and Germany since the mid-1980s. But, equally clearly, there is still some way to go to meet the convergence criteria however generously interpreted, and there is anxiety now that no further progress is being made.

Some of the problems of the Italian economy can be attributed to the divide between North and South. The industrial regions of the North are integrated into the economy of Europe and would benefit greatly from EMU. The South however is less advanced, presenting the same problems of development as confront Greece or Portugal. Whatever course is followed by Italy cannot be ideal for both of its two constituent parts. But the problems of the Italian economy are not just regional ones.

Perhaps the most fundamental question concerns Italian inflation. Over the past twenty years inflation in Italy has averaged 12 per cent a year, well above the EC average rate. Year-on-year price rises exceeded 20 per cent in 1974, and again in 1980. Even now the rate of inflation is about 6 per cent, with no clear evidence of a falling trend. (The contrast between Italian and French experience is brought out by Onofri and Tomasini, 1992.)

The latest devaluation of the lira was in January 1990. Short-term interest rates are about 2 percentage points higher for the lira than for the French franc or the D-Mark, suggesting that the market still thinks a moderate devaluation of the lira quite likely. As before, the option is usually discussed as 'just one more time' before exchange rates are finally locked together.

The market expectation is perhaps reinforced by recent experience of relative costs and prices. The prices of Italian goods which are exported, or which compete with imports in the home market, cannot get much out of line with those produced elsewhere in Europe. But the costs of non-traded goods and services continue to rise faster in Italy than elsewhere, and wages respond in an attempt to preserve living standards. Even the wages of those who work in the traded goods sector are affected, so the profit margins in that sector are subject to a progressively tighter squeeze. The process cannot continue for ever, at least in the private sector, because sooner or later the trading firms will be forced out of existence, or they will transfer their production out of Italy to another country where costs are lower or more stable.

In Italy, as in France, the transition to a lower rate of inflation in the 1980s seemed to require a significant rise in unemployment. Until the mid-1980s the rate of unemployment, measured on a comparable basis was always higher in Italy than in France, typically by a margin of about 2 percentage points. As both rates rose in parallel, the French caught up with the Italians so that around the peak in the mid-1980s both rates settled at about 10 per cent. (Since then the French rate has fallen back a little more than the rate in Italy.)

Statistical investigation of the relationship between wages and unemployment in Italy suggests that there were some detectable shifts in behaviour during the 1980s. Wage growth became more responsive to the pressure of demand, so that the rise in unemployment put a more effective brake on the inflationary spiral. Latterly however there is some suggestion that the effect is weakening again.

Ever since the 1950s wages in Italy have been set by a complicated process involving indexation. This means that an increase in prices leads automatically to higher wages, preserving living standards, but also giving a further boost to the rise in prices. The formula, which has changed many times, is called the *scala mobile*. During the 1970s the effectiveness of the indexation formula was increased, so that the tendency of inflation to persist was also increased. During the 1980s the process was put into reverse, and there is evidence that the Italian economy became less 'inflation-prone' as a result.

Now, the changes to the *scala mobile* were intended to complement the monetary policies required by membership of the EMS. Just as the exchange rate mechanism prevented the lira from responding at once and in proportion to the relative rise in Italian prices, so the modified wage indexation formula limited and delayed the response of labour costs. This is an excellent example of institutional or structural changes complementing and facilitating a change in monetary regime. It is probably these changes to the *scala mobile* which explain the favourable shift which can be detected in the relationship between unemployment and inflation in Italy in the 1980s.

Of course there is another side to these reforms. From the point of view of the workers directly involved the immediate effect was a fall of living standards and less certainty that the real value of pay would be maintained. Trade unions opposed the reforms. The Italian government would have liked to abolish the *scala mobile* altogether in 1990 but withdrew in the face of union opposition.

In 1985 the European Commission conducted a survey intended to identify the extent of 'employment rigidity' in different member states. One question asked was whether firms 'judged that there would be a positive employment impact from shorter redundancies and simpler legal procedures'; another question was whether firms expected 'a positive employment impact from measures facilitating periods of notice for temporary contracts'. The proportion of firms replying in the affirmative to both questions was higher in Italy than in any of the other EC countries (an average of 76 per cent in Italy as against 69 per cent in Germany, 51 per cent in France and just 28 per cent in the United Kingdom). These figures clearly demonstrate that the life of an employer in Italy can be a tiresome and frustrating one. Whether they tell us much about the reasons for the disappointing macroeconomic performance of the country is more doubtful (especially if one notes the high score recorded for Germany and the low score for the United Kingdom). The main macroeconomic problem of the Italian economy is not a lack of flexibility, but a lack of discipline, especially financial discipline in the public sector.

Even twenty years ago the Italian budget was in chronic imbalance, a problem which at that stage did not result from a high level of interest payments. Tax reforms have been introduced from time to time since then, which have helped to slow down the rise in the debt-to-national income ratio; but the reforms never went quite far enough. The difficulties have been political rather than economic or administrative. The budget could only be balanced by taking unpopular measures either on the tax or the spending side of the account. Perhaps successive governments have never felt sufficiently secure to grasp the nettle. More recently the situation has been made worse by the combination of persistently high unemployment, indexation of public sector pay and high nominal interest payments on an already-large stock of debt.

As a result of this history Italy is a long way from meeting either of the criteria in the Treaty for the level of public debt and for the scale of public borrowing. Steps are being taken to reduce borrowing, but some are of a purely temporary nature like the acceleration of receipts from VAT and corporate taxation. Longer-term plans centre on reducing tax evasion and substantial cuts in public spending. The size of debt interest is such that the rest of the budget needs to be in surplus by some 2 or 3 per cent of national income if the size of the debt is not to grow. At present the total deficit is some 10 per cent of income and the balance excluding interest is a deficit of some 2 per cent.

Privatisation may offer a relatively painless way of speeding up progress towards the Maastricht criteria. The proceeds of potential privatisation are estimated at 14-17 per cent of national income. The sale of public assets could directly reduce the gross debt of the public sector which is the definition on which attention is focussed in the Treaty. (The fact that the public sector is giving up an asset which should also have appeared in its balance sheet does not seem to have worried the drafters of the Treaty). The proceeds of privatisation could also be scored year-by-year against the budget deficit.

It is possible, on favourable assumptions, to set down a year-by-year progression for the Italian public sector deficit such that it is not too far out of line with the rest of Europe by the end of the decade. This would be consistent with a modest reduction in the level of debt, although the debt-to-national income ratio would still be much higher in Italy than in most other European countries. It is difficult to see how this could be done, however, without slowing down the growth of output and adding to unemployment.

If this profile for borrowing could be achieved the other member states would presumably welcome Italy into the EMU (provided of course that the other criteria were met). The actual problems that would be created in financial markets by the existence of a relatively large stock of Italian debt should not be exaggerated. The real dilemma for the Community as a whole arises if the borrowing of one of its member states appears to be out of control. Clearly the Community needs to be reassured that that is not the case with Italy.

The way that the criteria have been set the member states collectively will almost certainly have to pass judgement on the Italian case when the time comes to select the initial participants in EMU. The Italians will want to be members; and the Italian government will have used the fiscal criteria as a reason to introduce unpopular budgetary measures. The other countries will have to decide whether those measures go far enough. To get a sympathetic hearing the Italian authorities will have to be in a position to report success in combatting inflation. If they can do that, and also present a plausible plan to reduce debt further, then they may yet be amongst the founder-members of the EMU.

The United Kingdom

In the case of the United Kingdom we have to consider not just the readiness of the economy to become part of an EMU, but also the willingness of government and Parliament to accept the invitation if Britain was thought worthy to receive one. Britain was a late entrant to the European Economic Community. Having missed the opportunity to join the Common Market at the beginning, the British applied for membership in 1961 but were rejected because they wanted to revise the Rome Treaty in ways that were unacceptable to the existing members, especially the French. By 1970 the British position had modified substantially, and General de Gaulle had resigned. In 1973 Britain became a member, although even then the terms of entry had to be renegotiated after the change of government the following year.

Britain was also a late entrant into the exchange rate mechanism of the EMS. Although technically Britain was a member of the EMS from the start, the pound was in fact floating independently until 1990 when, with some show of reluctance, Britain joined the ERM, whilst allowing a wide margin for fluctuation about the central rate for sterling. In much the same spirit Britain initially opposed EMU and threatened to block its progress, and then at Maastricht secured a unique right to opt out of the third stage (as well as opting out of the harmonisation of social policies). With this history in mind it is not difficult to imagine EMU going ahead towards the end of this decade without British participation. If subsequent events ran true to form Britain would change its mind a few years later, have one last try at rewriting the rules of the club, but finally decide to join it.

It is possible, nevertheless, that the British will behave differently this time. The original reluctance to join the European Community was largely due to the strength of the links, both economic and political, which tied Britain to North America and the Commonwealth. That connection is still in place, but its influence has been gradually eroded. British trade links with the rest of Europe have developed rapidly and the political significance of Britain's 'special relationship' with the United States is much less than it was twenty, or even ten, years ago. Both industry and the City are anxious that they should compete on equal terms in the markets of Europe. Trade unionists see advantage in the European Social Charter and, in some cases, would like to imitate the German model of collective bargaining. There is a general awareness in Britain, as in France, that domestic economic policy has met with little success, and that in this respect shared responsibility might be better than independence.

Taking a long-term comparison, the performance of the British economy does not look very good set alongside the European average. In the last twenty years inflation in Britain averaged 9.7 per cent a year, compared with 8.2 per cent a year for the European Community as a whole. The rate varied a lot from year to year, being well over 20 per cent in 1975, and rising to another peak in 1980. By the mid-1980s the rate was down to 5 per cent a year (or lower on some measures) although at the end of the decade it speeded up again for a few years, as high as 10 per cent on one measure at one stage. There is no doubt the economy is still 'inflation-prone' and that the commitment to a medium-term financial strategy was not enough to overcome that weakness.

The United Kingdom has experienced the same upward trend in unemployment as the rest of Europe. The increase was most rapid in the early 1980s following the sharp recession of 1980-81, the strong appreciation of the real exchange rate and the new economic policies introduced by the Conservative government. At its peak in 1986 unemployment was a little higher in Britain than in either France or Italy. Subsequently it fell sharply during the boom at the end of the 1980s but it is now rising again as a consequence of the recession.

The increase in unemployment between the 1970s and the 1980s is probably the main explanation for the improvement in inflation performance. About the same time there were important changes in policy towards the labour market, notably the end of incomes policy and new rules limiting the activities of trade unions. These and related changes undoubtedly made the labour market more 'flexible', but there is no clear evidence that it has become any easier to reconcile low inflation with low unemployment. It is, of course, too early to say whether membership of the exchange rate mechanism has improved that relationship.

The United Kingdom would have little difficulty in meeting the criteria for fiscal rectitude if the test was based on its performance over the last five years. In 1988 and 1989 the financial balance of general government was actually in surplus, and the ratio of public debt to national income was falling for most of the 1970s and 1980s. That ratio, which was exceptionally high at the end of the war is now below the European average — thanks partly to the erosion of the debt in the 1970s by high inflation and negative real interest rates. The budget surpluses of the late 1980s were due partly to the strong growth of the economy, partly to revenue from North Sea oil production.

The fact that the United Kingdom is a significant oil producer has clearly had an effect on economic policies and performance in the 1980s. The decision to stay outside the ERM was partly explained by the status of sterling as a petro-currency. The appreciation of the real exchange rate around the end of the 1970s may be explained in part by the rise in oil prices, although the fall in oil prices in 1986 did not seem to have a comparable effect. The possibility remains that a large-scale upset in the world market for oil could affect the British economy and the rest of Europe in different and opposing ways. This could, at some stage, make the position of the United Kingdom in an EMU uncomfortable. With exchange rates fixed the main effect would be felt on the balance of payments and on public sector revenue. But these effects would be relatively easy to recognise and to quantify, so it should not be too difficult to abstract from them in assessing the financial position of the rest of the economy. Indeed the British economy might even be better able to weather the storms of the oil market if its exchange rate was fixed irrevocably as part of EMU.

The British economy is also unlike the rest of Europe in having a relatively small agricultural sector, just 2 per cent of total employment, compared to 6 per cent in France and 9 per cent in Italy. This difference contributes to the long history of disputes about agricultural policy in the Community and about Britain's contribution to the Community budget. In this area at least British interests suggest a much more liberal attitude towards market forces than has been shown by the Community since its foundation.

In other areas the British commitment to the free market is more recent. The reforms of the 1980s have created an economic system in Britain more 'flexible' and 'market-orientated' in many respects than the rest of Europe. Britain has been ahead of the trend in lifting credit controls, exchange controls and trade restrictions, in privatisation and in deregulation. The models for these reforms have been American rather than European. It may be that the rest of Europe will follow the same route in due course, but it is also possible that assimilation of Britain to the European norm could involve introducing new regulation in some areas, credit control for example, and perhaps the labour market as well.

London is, of course, a major world financial centre, thanks partly to its liberal regulatory regime. The ambition of the City to be the financial capital of Europe, and the site of the new central banking operations, provides an important incentive for British participation in EMU. It may even prove to be the decisive factor. Granting independence to the Bank of England would be a very strong signal to that effect.

For the economy as a whole the transition to EMU would not be an easy one. The current recession is not directly caused by European economic integration or by membership of the exchange rate mechanism, but if Britain is to make a success of participation in an EMU, then the British must learn to cope with situations of this kind without having recourse to devaluation or unilateral cuts in interest rates. It remains to be seen how this will be done.

It also remains to be seen whether the United Kingdom economy will in fact pass all the tests of the convergence criteria when the day of reckoning comes. If the answers are on the borderline, the other member states may well decide that Britain should be a late-comer to the EMU, as to so much else in Europe.

Spain

Total national income per head of population in Spain is about two-thirds that of Italy or the United Kingdom. The proportion of the labour force employed in agriculture is 13 per cent, which is double that in France. The Spanish economy is in the process of transition, catching-up with living standards elsewhere in Europe, opening up new trade and financial links and removing barriers to market forces.

Spain first applied for membership of the European Economic Community in 1977 after the introduction of multi-party democracy. Negotiations took a long time, but Spain was admitted to membership in 1986, with transitional arrangements continuing especially with respect to agriculture. In 1989 Spain also joined the exchange rate mechanism of the EMS, although with wide exchange rate bands. (Spanish policy and its effects on inflation are described in Larre and Torres, 1992.)

The experience of inflation in Spain is similar to that in Italy. The average annual rate for both countries over the last twenty years is 12.3 per cent, and the peak annual rate in both countries has been over 20 per cent. In both countries inflation was progressively reduced in the 1980s, and in both countries it has been running recently at about 6 per cent a year. In Spain, as in Italy, the rate of increase in the price of non-traded goods is especially rapid. In Spain, to a greater extent than in Italy, this may be explained as the consequence of rising living standards and output per head. (The process of economic development is accompanied by higher rents and by higher prices of services — say, orchestral concerts — in which productivity growth is impossible.)

Until the late 1970s the unemployment rate was also similar in Spain and in Italy. In the 1980s however unemployment rose exceptionally fast in Spain, to reach over 20 per cent of the labour force in 1985, the highest rate in Europe. Employment fell every year from 1975 to 1985, with the largest falls concentrated in agriculture. Participation rates, already low, fell further and long-term unemployment became a severe social problem. Spanish unemployment is still the highest in (Western) Europe, although it has now eased back to about 15 per cent.

Possibly this dramatic rise was necessary to slow down inflation, but if so the 'cost ratio' was exceptionally high in Spain. An alternative interpretation would be that unemployment in Spain falls into the same category as unemployment in Eastern Europe — a symptom of rapid transformation. If so the main cause of the slowdown in Spanish inflation was the slow growth of import prices helped by the strength of the peseta.

The peseta has been strong despite a sizeable deficit on the current account of the balance of payments, thanks to a vigorous inflow of capital, attracted to Spain by its relatively low wage costs, and by progressive liberalisation. The experience of Spain since joining the European Community is, in most respects, an excellent advertisement for the benefits of membership. Certainly that experience contrasts very favourably with the ten years that preceded entry.

It is another question whether Spain is ready to participate in an EMU. Since 1985 the ratio of public debt to total income has stabilised at a level similar to that in France or Germany. The scale of government borrowing is a little on the high side, but much lower than in Italy. The main question, so far as convergence is concerned, must be about inflationary pressure, especially in the context of such a high rate of unemployment. But if the Spanish authorities are prepared to accept relatively slow growth for most of the 1990s, so that the pressure of demand in labour markets remains low, the criterion on inflation could well be met.

It would be a strange outcome in many ways if Spain were to be accepted into EMU whilst Italy, a founder member of the European Common Market, was rejected. So far as the simple arithmetic is concerned that could easily happen. In political terms it is less easy to contemplate.

The Netherlands

In many respects the Netherlands is already in a monetary union with Germany. If EMU takes place at all it is very hard to imagine it taking place without the Dutch. Their experience can indeed be used as an indication of what life might be like for other countries in EMU at a later date. (For a description of the Dutch experience see in't Veld, 1992.)

This is a relatively small open economy, with output per person employed high by international standards but output per head of the population rather lower than in France or (West) Germany thanks to an unusually low participation rate. Trading links with Germany are of the first importance.

The exchange rate between the guilder and the D-Mark was almost fixed for a long time before the EMS was set up. The Netherlands stayed in the 'snake' — the currency band — for most of the 1970s. Within the EMS the guilder has been devalued against the D-Mark on only two occasions, in 1979 and in 1983, by just 2 per cent each time. Short-term interest rates are now almost identical in the two countries.

Over the last twenty years as a whole the rate of inflation has been a little higher in the Netherlands than in Germany, about 5 per cent as against about 4 per cent. Since the early 1980s however the rate in the two countries has been almost the same every year, with the Dutch rate below the German on many occasions.

The rate of unemployment is rather higher in the Netherlands than in (West) Germany. It would be difficult now to see this as the cost of reducing inflation, since inflation has been low and fairly constant in both countries for the best part of a decade. An alternative, more plausible interpretation, would be that the sustainable rate of unemployment is rather higher in Netherlands for structural reasons. One such reason may be the relative generosity of social security provision, which is also reflected in an exceptionally large number of disability pensioners. Although some would argue that the social security provision in the Netherlands is too generous, there is no reason why it has to be changed if that is the arrangement that the Dutch people prefer — and if they accept the consequences. This structural difference has not disrupted in any way their close monetary relationship with Germany.

The question of the Dutch public finances is a related one. The ratio of debt to national income and the scale of public borrowing in the Netherlands may both be 'excessive' according to the Maastricht Treaty protocol. The Dutch have a history of relatively high public spending, not unconnected with their social security provision. (In assessing the debt position it should be remembered however that the public sector pension scheme in the Netherlands is a funded one.) If this fiscal extravagance was a real problem for the financial markets or for monetary management one might expect to see interest rates higher in the Netherlands than in Germany. In fact the margin between the long-term interest rates is less than per cent. If it worries the markets so little, it is not clear why the Dutch debt position should worry the central bankers of Europe as they move towards monetary union.

Belgium and Luxembourg

The Belgian economy is not quite as closely linked to Germany as is the Dutch economy. The share of Belgian exports going to France is larger than the share going to Germany by a small margin (21 per cent as against

108 *Achieving Monetary Union in Europe*

20 per cent). The history of Belgian involvement in the EMS is rather different from the Dutch, possibly because of closer links with France. Like the Netherlands, Belgium had remained in the 'snake' currency bands for most of the 1970s. Initially in the EMS the Belgian franc stayed in line with the guilder. In the realignments from 1981 to 1987 however the Belgian franc was always devalued against the D-Mark and against the guilder. The net effect of various changes in 1981 and 1982 was in fact for the Belgian franc to keep roughly in line with the French franc.

The average rate of inflation in Belgium over the past twenty years is just under 6 per cent (the same in Luxembourg) about 1 per cent higher than in the Netherlands. The most striking difference perhaps was in the early 1980s when for several years the rate of inflation was much higher in Belgium (and in France) than it was in the Netherlands (and in Germany). To what extent this was the result, rather than the cause, of their different use of EMS membership is a difficult issue to decide. An important role was also assigned in the case of Belgium to an explicit incomes policy that linked pay to a competitiveness norm. The fixing of the exchange rate was backed up by a determined effort to ensure that its implications for wage setting could not be ignored.

In 1990 the Belgian authorities announced their intention of pegging the Belgian franc to the stronger currencies in the ERM, saying that they would preserve the parity with the D-Mark in the event of a realignment. Since then the franc has been kept inside a very narrow band of per cent each side of the central rate against the D-Mark. The consequence has been that the short-term interest-rate differential against the D-Mark (previously about 1 per cent) has virtually disappeared. Long-term interest rates still show a small margin, perhaps because of the very large stock of public sector debt outstanding.

The gross public debt of Belgium is nearly 130 per cent of national income, more than twice the 'ceiling' of 60 per cent laid down in the Maastricht Treaty. The budget deficit is around 6 per cent of national income, also about double the figure in the protocol. The position on the stock of debt (but not on the rate of borrowing) appears indeed to be considerably more serious in Belgium than in Italy or the Netherlands, but at least the debt-to-income ratio is not actually rising in Belgium anymore. Projections by the European Commission suggest that it will remain virtually constant for the next two years. It would, of course, be impossible at that rate for the strict convergence criterion to be met within the likely timetable for the transition to EMU.

The problem for the Belgian government is that interest payments on the debt are accounting for about a quarter of government revenue. Clearly that situation would be eased if interest rates in Europe generally were to fall, but this remains at best a remote prospect. The Belgians will therefore have higher taxation or lower public spending of other kinds than their neighbours elsewhere in Europe for the foreseeable future. It is not clear however that this misfortune is a good reason for excluding Belgium (and presumably Luxembourg as well) from participating in EMU.

Denmark

The Danish economy is small but prosperous, with output per head of the population similar to that in (West) Germany. The agricultural sector is rather larger than in Germany, but still employs under 6 per cent of the labour force. There are well-established trade links with Germany and also with the United Kingdom. (The whole of the European Community accounts for only just over one half of Danish exports.)

Denmark applied unsuccessfully to join the Community in the 1960s alongside the United Kingdom. When Britain re-applied in 1967 so did Denmark, and in 1973 Denmark was also admitted. This linkage of the two applications was mainly due to the importance to Denmark of the British market for food.

Subsequently the history of Danish involvement with Europe has not followed the British pattern. The Danes stayed with the 'snake' currency agreement after Britain dropped out. The Danes also participated in the exchange rate mechanism of the EMS, although initially the Kroner was frequently devalued.

Over the past twenty years inflation in Denmark has averaged 8.2 per cent a year, which is also the rate for the European Community as a whole. Since the change of government in 1982 the emphasis of policy has been more on reducing inflation than it had been before, and by 1990 the rate was down to just 2 per cent.

Unemployment in Denmark followed the common European pattern of a steeply rising trend from the mid-1970s to the mid-1980s, when it reached about 10 per cent. This is in marked contrast with the neighbouring countries, Norway and Sweden, where unemployment remained exceptionally low right up to the end of the 1980s. Statistical studies suggest that this rise in unemployment in Denmark played an important part in slowing down inflation. Changes in the structure of the labour market in the 1980s, especially the ending of automatic price indexation, may have increased the responsiveness of wages to the pressure of demand.

The most persistent problem of the Danish economy has been the deficit on the current account of the balance of payments, which persisted for an unbroken run of 26 years until 1990. It can be attributed to unusually low savings rather than unusually high investment. The legacy is an exceptionally large foreign debt.

Balance of payments problems have been little discussed during the negotiations of the Maastricht Treaty, perhaps because they are not particularly acute for any member state at the present time. In practice however it will probably be necessary for each member state to balance its external accounts approximately over a run of years. The Danish record of persistent international borrowing for a generation would be called into question sooner or later if it were repeated within an EMU.

To offset the low savings of the private sector the Danish government ran a public sector surplus for the three years 1986-88. The tightening of fiscal policy in the early 1980s was accompanied by a period of quite rapid growth. Some commentators have seen the causation as running from fiscal rectitude through improved public confidence to increased economic activity. It has been called an 'expansionary fiscal contraction', but the evidence is not conclusive. Another interpretation would be that faster growth made a fiscal surplus possible. The suggestion, drawn from the Danish case, that more heavily indebted governments as in Italy, the Netherlands or Belgium could expect faster growth as a result of raising taxes should be viewed with some scepticism.

If the Danish economy maintains its recent performance it should have little difficulty in passing the entrance examination for EMU. Indeed the example of Denmark will probably be held up as the right one for Sweden and Norway to follow if they too want to join the Community. But the Danish experience includes a high rate of unemployment which the other Scandinavian countries still hope to avoid.

Greece

Greece was two years ahead of Spain and Portugal in applying for membership of the European Community in the mid-1970s after the fall of the three dictatorships. Greece became a member in 1981, thanks partly to the energetic support of the French government. As with most other new members quite lengthy transitional arrangements were agreed.

Output per head of the population in Greece is lower than in any other member state if calculated at current exchange rates (broadly the same as in Portugal if calculated using indices of purchasing power). The agricultural sector accounts for more than a quarter of total employment — the highest of any member state.

Over the past twenty years the rate of inflation in Greece has averaged 16 per cent, and in 1990 it was just over 20 per cent, much higher than in any other member state of the Community. Until the late 1970s the experience of inflation in Greece was not very different from that in several other countries of Europe. The rate was over 20 per cent in 1974, but the same was true of Italy and Portugal (and also of Japan). In the late 1970s the rate eased back in Greece as elsewhere, and the re-acceleration to 22 per cent in 1980 was not very different from the experience of Italy or of the United Kingdom. But after the early 1980s, when most European countries succeeded at about the same time in cutting inflation right back at least into single figures, the rate in Greece remained in the range 15-20 per cent year after year.

Despite this high rate of inflation, Greece was not spared from the general rise in unemployment, although the level stayed below the European average — and far below the exceptionally high rate endured in Spain.

The drachma does not participate in the exchange rate mechanism and continues to depreciate rapidly each year against the ecu. Short-term interest rates in 1991 averaged 21.7 per cent in Greece compared with 11 per cent for the Community as a whole.

Greece would also at present fail the tests of fiscal policy convergence. Government borrowing is 18 per cent of national income, with the stock of debt 96 per cent, and rising.

There seems little if any chance of Greece meeting the Maastricht convergence criteria within a reasonable timetable. It is also unlikely that the other member states would wish to make an exception in its favour. It is indeed doubtful whether the best interests of the Greek economy would be served by participating in an EMU at the present stage of reform and development.

Portugal

In 1960 Portugal joined EFTA rather than the EEC. Full membership of the European Community was not possible until effective democracy was restored in the mid-1970s. Even then the negotiations took a long time for Portugal, as for Spain, because the Community budget was in no position to stand the extra cost of members who would be net beneficiaries. Portugal, along with Spain, became a full member in 1986.

Output per head of the population in Portugal is only about half that of Spain, if measured at current exchange rates (although it is about 70 per cent in terms of estimated purchasing power). Living standards are similar to those in Greece. About 20 per cent of the workforce is employed in agriculture.

Over the past twenty years the rate of inflation has averaged about 17 per cent a year, similar to the rate in Greece. After the revolution of 1974 the new government did not give high priority to containing inflation and the rate remained over 20 per cent continuously from 1977-84. About the time that Portugal joined the Community the rate of inflation slowed down, as low as 10 per cent in 1987 and 1988, but in the last few years it has re-accelerated a little.

Unemployment in Portugal is very low compared with Spain, and well below the Community average. In 1991 the rate was just under 4 per cent, making it lower than in any other member state (except Luxembourg). Unemployment has indeed been falling since the mid-1980s; but the economy is showing signs of overheating and it is doubtful whether such a good unemployment record could be maintained at the same time as the rate of inflation is brought down.

Portugal is not yet a member of the exchange-rate mechanism, but it is the intention of the government to join as soon as possible. Until 1988 the exchange rate of the escudo depreciated substantially each year. In 1989 the fall against the ecu was just 2 per cent, despite continuing rapid inflation and in 1991 the exchange rate actually appreciated. As with the Spanish peseta, this buoyancy reflects capital inflows attracted by high nominal interest rates and opportunities to participate in economic development.

In 1990 a new adjustment plan was adopted, with the acronym QUANTUM, intended to chart the path to participation in EMU. To qualify for EMU member states will need to keep their currencies within the 'narrow band option' of the exchange rate mechanism. The plan involves bringing the Portuguese rate of inflation down to the Community average by 1995. Given past history this is an ambitious goal, and progress so far is not altogether encouraging. The latest OECD forecasts show inflation at 10 per cent in 1992 and 10 per cent in 1993.

Portugal might also have some difficulty in meeting the convergence criteria for public sector borrowing. In recent years borrowing has been around 4 or 5 per cent of national income, whilst gross debt is approaching 80 per cent. For a developing economy these figures may not be unreasonable, but they would be a sufficient reason on their own for excluding Portugal from EMU if the Treaty criteria are given a strict interpretation. But as with several other member states the main issue will be inflation, not debt.

Ireland

Finally we turn to Ireland, which must be a serious candidate for full participation in EMU from the start. (See also Bradley and Whelan, 1992.)

Ireland joined the European Community in 1973 together with the United Kingdom, but more recently it has followed distinctly different economic policies from those of its larger neighbour. Ireland joined the exchange rate mechanism in 1979, breaking the link between the pound sterling and the Irish pound. This was expected to produce a relatively rapid convergence on the low-inflation, low-interest-rate pattern of Germany, rather than the high-inflation, high-interest-rate pattern of the United Kingdom. Ironically the effect of breaking the link with sterling was to cut the Irish pound off from the *appreciation* of sterling associated with the oil price rise and the change of government in Britain.

In a small open economy like Ireland the rate of inflation is very dependent on the exchange rate and on world prices. The central rate of the Irish pound in the EMS has been changed on only three occasions: a devaluation of 3 per cent in 1983, a revaluation of 2 per cent in 1985 and a devaluation of 8 per cent in 1986. The rate of inflation has been low since the mid-1980s, and recently has been one of the lowest in Europe. This is in contrast with earlier years: over the last twenty years Irish inflation has averaged 10.9 per cent compared with 8.2 per cent for the EC as a whole. The recent performance of the Irish economy is impressive, and may be held up as a model for successful adjustment towards EMU. But serious underlying problems remain. The ratio of public debt to national income is very high, higher indeed than in the Netherlands or Italy. Because of the higher level of interest payments which that implies the level of government borrowing is also above the Community average.

The very high level of unemployment (about 16 per cent) makes Ireland a difficult model to recommend. If this is the social cost of achieving price stability, not everyone will consider it worth paying. In the context of a very open economy however that interpretation can be challenged. The only way to create more jobs in that context is by improving competitiveness. The attempt to do that by exchange depreciation would soon be frustrated by wage increases, by a higher level of interest rates and by a reduced inflow of foreign capital. If this is correct, unemployment must be tackled by some other means.

Conclusions

The member states of the European Community exhibit a rich variety of structure and macroeconomic experience. It is easy to become fascinated by a mass of detail and lose sight of the main issues which will determine whether EMU takes place as intended, and how successful it will prove in the long run.

The first requirement is that the rate of inflation is low in both Germany and France, at least as low as it is now, and preferably several percentage points lower. The experience of the past five years suggests that this is quite possible to maintain, although experience in earlier periods warns that it is by no means inevitable. In the short run, that is during the countdown to EMU, success in this respect depends in part on good luck with the international environment, in part on the determination of the monetary authorities in both countries. Progress towards political union will also be crucial. In the long run the system will not work well unless there is a convergence of economic institutions and behaviour. This will involve a break with tradition in both countries, but more so in France than in (West) Germany.

If Germany and France are both ready to join EMU then it should not be difficult to assemble enough other member states to form the required quorum. The Netherlands, Belgium, Luxembourg and Denmark are all likely to be available, provided a generous view is taken of the criteria on public finance. If Austria is a member of the Community by the time EMU is formed, that would provide another strong candidate. Ireland would be a possibility too, whether the United Kingdom was in or out.

Having got that far, the difficult decision would concern the southern

114 *Achieving Monetary Union in Europe*

tier, including Italy as well as Spain, Portugal and Greece. If the decision were being taken now, it is possible that they would all be excluded on the grounds that they remain too prone to inflation. But experience shows that reforms can be introduced successfully if there is sufficient incentive to do so, and the judgement could be quite different towards the end of the decade.

The timing of British participation is a less important issue for the community as a whole. If EMU is a success the British will eventually want to join it. If necessary the venture can go ahead perfectly well without them.

Table 1 *Changes in EMS central rates (per cent change in central rate)*

Dates of realignments	Belgian franc	Danish kroner	German mark	French franc	Irish punt	Italian lira	Dutch guilder
24/09/1979	0.0	−2.9	+2.0	0.0	0.0	0.0	0.0
31/11/1979	0.0	−4.8	0.0	0.0	0.0	0.0	0.0
02/03/1981	0.0	0.0	0.0	0.0	0.0	−6.0	0.0
05/10/1981	0.0	0.0	+5.5	−3.0	0.0	−3.0	+5.5
22/02/1982	−8.5	−3.0	0.0	0.0	0.0	0.0	0.0
14/06/1982	0.0	0.0	+4.25	−5.75	0.0	−2.75	+4.25
21/03/1983	+1.5	+2.5	+5.5	−2.5	−3.5	−2.5	+3.5
21/07/1985	+2.0	+2.0	+2.0	+2.0	+2.0	−6.0	+2.0
07/04/1986	+1.0	+1.0	+3.0	−3.0	0.0	0.0	+3.0
04/08/1986	0.0	0.0	0.0	0.0	−8.0	0.0	0.0
12/01/1987	+2.0	0.0	+3.0	0.0	0.0	0.0	+3.0
08/01/1990	0.0	0.0	0.0	0.0	0.0	−3.7	0.0

Table 2 *Consumers' expenditure deflators (per cent rate of change over previous year)*

	Germany	Netherlands	Belgium	Austria	France	Denmark
1978	2.75	4.56	4.21	4.10	9.18	9.21
1979	4.28	4.36	3.89	4.59	10.79	10.51
1980	5.78	7.07	6.29	6.40	13.25	10.62
1981	6.43	6.30	8.59	7.55	13.00	12.00
1982	5.25	5.27	7.91	6.03	11.59	10.27
1983	3.36	2.77	6.97	3.41	9.67	6.80
1984	2.73	2.17	6.07	5.60	7.66	6.37
1985	2.04	2.21	5.93	3.31	5.78	4.35
1986	−0.50	0.33	0.70	1.92	2.67	2.87
1987	0.60	−0.17	1.69	0.90	3.15	4.58
1988	1.40	0.67	1.37	1.60	2.64	4.89
1989	3.05	2.06	3.37	2.72	3.45	5.02
1990	2.49	2.43	3.45	3.16	2.94	2.59
1991(a)	3.70	2.69	3.33	3.81	3.10	2.81

	Ireland	Italy	UK	Spain	Portugal	Greece
1978	7.96	13.28	9.09	18.90	20.60	12.80
1979	14.75	14.34	13.52	16.58	24.30	16.60
1980	18.67	20.63	16.31	16.55	21.40	22.00
1981	19.63	18.10	11.22	14.30	20.40	22.40
1982	14.99	16.93	8.70	14.61	21.00	20.70
1983	9.10	15.13	4.76	12.29	25.80	18.10
1984	7.44	11.82	5.09	10.88	28.10	17.90
1985	4.93	9.00	5.37	8.22	19.60	18.20
1986	4.30	5.78	4.40	8.78	14.70	22.20
1987	3.26	5.02	4.31	5.36	8.60	15.50
1988	2.51	5.29	5.05	5.14	10.10	14.20
1989	3.89	6.26	5.59	6.72	13.00	14.70
1990	3.23	6.23	4.72	6.70	13.40	20.00
1991(a)	3.04	6.70	5.40	6.07	11.50	17.50

Source: *NIESR database and Datastream.*
(a) *Includes forecast.*

Table 3 Unit labour costs (per cent rate of change over previous year)

	Germany	Netherlands	Belgium	Austria	France	Denmark
1978	3.15	5.73	3.81	9.43	9.52	9.31
1979	3.98	5.18	5.51	1.84	9.88	7.96
1980	7.66	5.50	4.28	5.13	13.67	10.63
1981	4.74	2.61	6.29	8.31	12.50	9.15
1982	4.19	4.44	3.62	3.53	11.67	9.66
1983	0.22	−0.30	3.03	2.12	9.19	6.35
1984	0.65	−2.95	4.75	3.92	5.77	3.41
1985	1.94	0.63	4.75	3.44	4.47	3.65
1986	2.96	1.77	2.47	4.93	2.30	3.98
1987	2.67	2.25	0.60	2.15	2.04	9.29
1988	0.30	0.30	−1.20	−0.10	1.30	1.90
1989	0.60	−1.60	1.32	2.40	2.67	1.77
1990	2.87	2.63	3.60	3.13	3.46	1.16
1991(a)	4.72	3.16	3.86	4.08	3.90	1.81

	Ireland	Italy	UK	Spain	Portugal	Greece
1978	13.20	11.99	10.38	21.08	20.63	16.20
1979	20.98	14.65	14.01	16.71	15.35	20.68
1980	20.99	17.94	21.04	11.90	22.43	18.73
1981	15.40	20.63	9.74	12.25	20.80	23.49
1982	14.88	15.89	4.56	11.88	19.79	28.26
1983	11.08	13.86	3.39	10.90	19.96	19.22
1984	6.01	8.38	4.22	4.79	18.25	18.91
1985	5.10	8.82	4.39	6.05	19.21	20.95
1986	7.44	5.33	4.09	9.66	14.34	10.44
1987	0.40	5.37	3.52	6.16	10.98	11.23
1988	3.20	5.60	6.80	5.60	15.40	18.40
1989	−0.29	6.16	8.99	7.77	12.30	15.96
1990	1.75	9.63	11.25	8.70	14.97	22.14
1991(a)	3.53	7.00	6.64	6.79	15.17	13.50

Source: *NIESR database and Datastream.*
(a) *Includes forecast.*

Table 4 *Long-term interest rates (per cent)*

	Germany	Netherlands	Belgium	Austria	France	Denmark
1978	6.13	7.74	8.45	8.21	10.61	17.46
1979	7.58	8.78	9.70	7.96	10.85	17.41
1980	8.45	10.19	12.20	9.32	13.78	19.14
1981	10.13	11.52	13.78	10.61	16.29	19.29
1982	8.94	9.93	13.45	9.92	16.00	20.46
1983	8.07	8.23	11.80	8.17	14.37	14.40
1984	7.98	8.10	11.96	8.02	13.40	14.04
1985	7.04	7.33	10.61	7.77	11.87	11.57
1986	6.17	6.36	7.93	7.33	9.12	10.55
1987	6.24	6.35	7.83	6.94	10.22	11.92
1988	6.48	6.10	7.85	6.67	9.22	10.60
1989	7.03	7.21	8.64	7.13	9.15	10.22
1990	8.82	8.99	10.06	8.74	10.42	10.98
1991(a)	8.50	8.90	9.60	8.60	9.60	10.00

	Ireland	Italy	UK	Spain	Portugal	Greece
1978	12.83	13.05	12.07	11.93	19.33	11.08
1979	15.07	13.02	12.95	13.31	20.50	13.08
1980	15.35	15.25	13.91	15.96	20.50	16.75
1981	17.27	19.36	14.88	15.81	20.90	18.00
1982	17.06	20.22	13.09	15.99	23.83	16.00
1983	13.90	18.30	11.27	16.91	28.83	18.00
1984	14.61	15.60	11.27	16.52	31.50	18.00
1985	12.64	13.71	11.06	13.37	30.13	18.00
1986	11.06	11.47	10.06	11.36	22.50	18.00
1987	11.27	10.58	9.59	12.77	19.06	18.04
1988	9.49	10.54	9.67	11.74	17.20	18.73
1989	8.95	11.61	10.19	13.80	19.75	20.38
1990	10.09	11.88	11.81	14.60	21.70	25.30
1991(a)	9.50	11.50	10.05	13.10	22.10	25.80

Source: *NIESR database and Datastream.*
(a) *Includes forecast.*

118 Achieving Monetary Union in Europe

Table 5 Unemployment rates [a] (per cent of labour force)

	Germany	Netherlands	Belgium	Austria	France	Denmark
1978	3.15	3.43	7.24	1.71	5.34	7.29
1979	2.85	3.49	7.50	1.73	5.99	6.19
1980	2.52	4.13	7.89	1.54	6.33	7.00
1981	3.40	6.26	10.16	2.10	7.50	9.16
1982	5.02	8.82	11.89	3.11	8.15	9.79
1983	6.62	11.16	13.17	3.68	8.36	10.44
1984	7.08	11.18	13.21	3.79	9.80	10.06
1985	7.17	10.05	12.31	3.61	10.21	9.05
1986	6.44	9.18	11.63	3.11	10.39	7.82
1987	6.19	8.66	11.32	3.80	10.50	7.83
1988	6.16	8.28	10.28	3.58	9.99	8.59
1989	5.61	7.37	9.29	3.16	9.41	9.32
1990	5.07	6.47	8.79	3.30	9.01	9.58
1991(a)	4.99	6.46	8.84	3.54	9.43	9.79

	Ireland	Italy	UK	Spain	Portugal	Greece
1978	8.19	7.29	4.92	6.96	7.92	1.83
1979	7.14	7.76	4.54	8.64	8.19	1.90
1980	7.30	7.66	6.10	11.46	7.98	2.75
1981	9.91	8.53	9.05	14.32	7.66	4.05
1982	11.42	9.19	10.43	16.41	7.50	5.78
1983	14.00	10.03	11.25	18.20	7.89	7.84
1984	15.53	10.14	11.40	20.15	8.55	8.15
1985	17.36	10.19	11.60	21.46	8.69	7.79
1986	17.36	11.24	11.76	21.03	8.59	7.38
1987	17.51	12.09	10.35	20.51	7.13	7.36
1988	16.72	12.17	8.18	19.49	5.75	7.68
1989	15.64	12.09	6.19	17.27	5.03	7.49
1990	14.05	11.04	5.52	16.25	4.63	7.74
1991(a)	14.72	11.30	8.22	15.92	4.50	9.00

[a] Commonly used definitions of unemployment rates.
[b] Includes forecast.

The Member States 119

Chart 1 *Inflation rates in Europe*

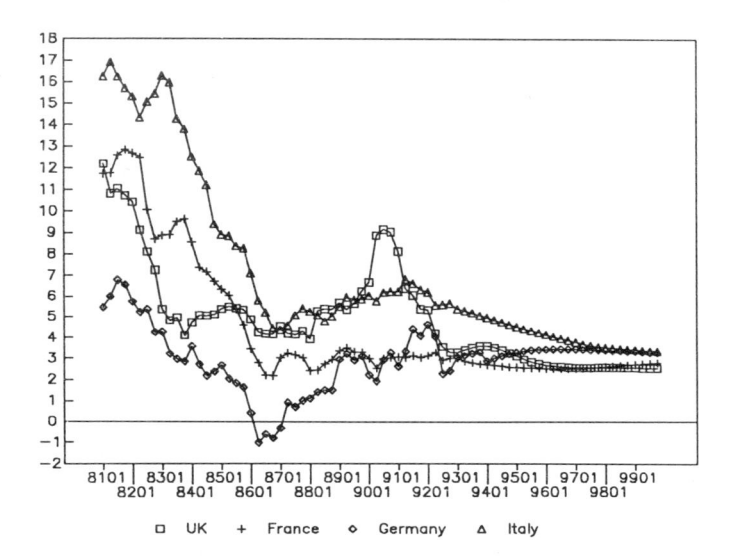

□ UK + France ◇ Germany △ Italy

Chart 2 *Budget deficits in Europe*

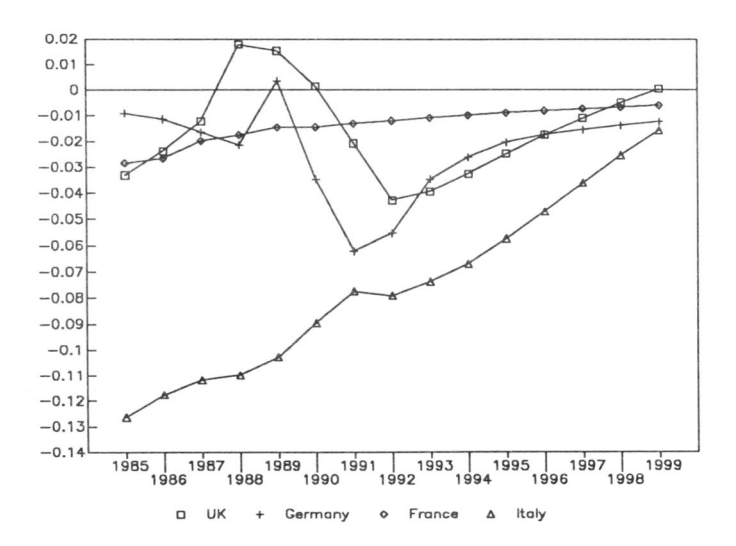

□ UK + Germany ◇ France △ Italy

120 *Achieving Monetary Union in Europe*

Chart 3   *Current balances in Europe*

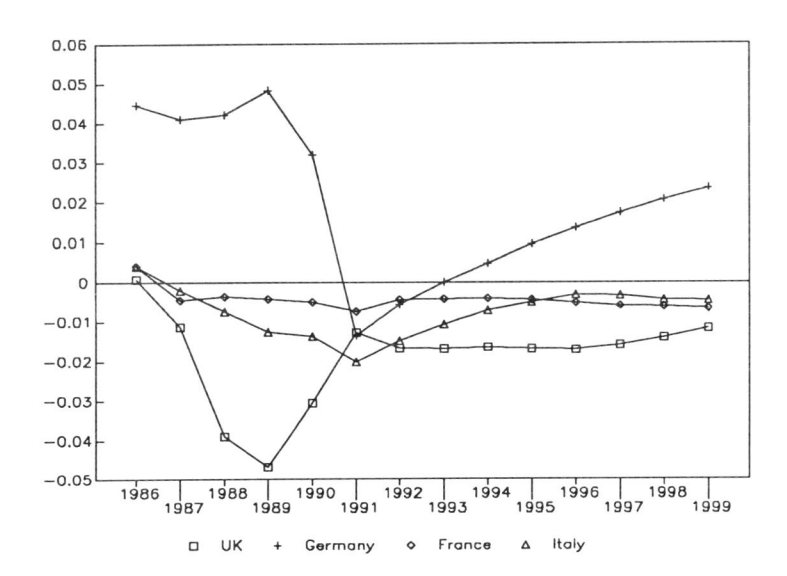

Chart 4   *Unemployment in Europe*

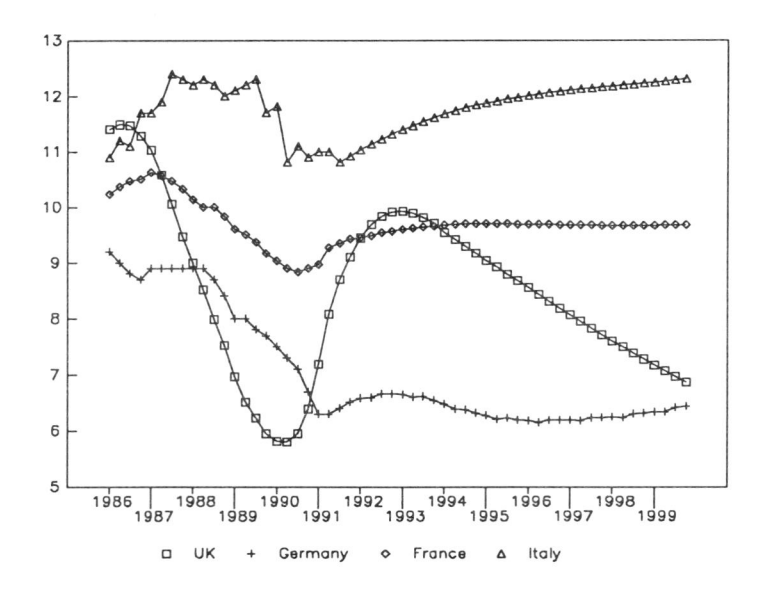

Chart 5a *Short-term interest rates for Germany, the Netherlands and Austria*

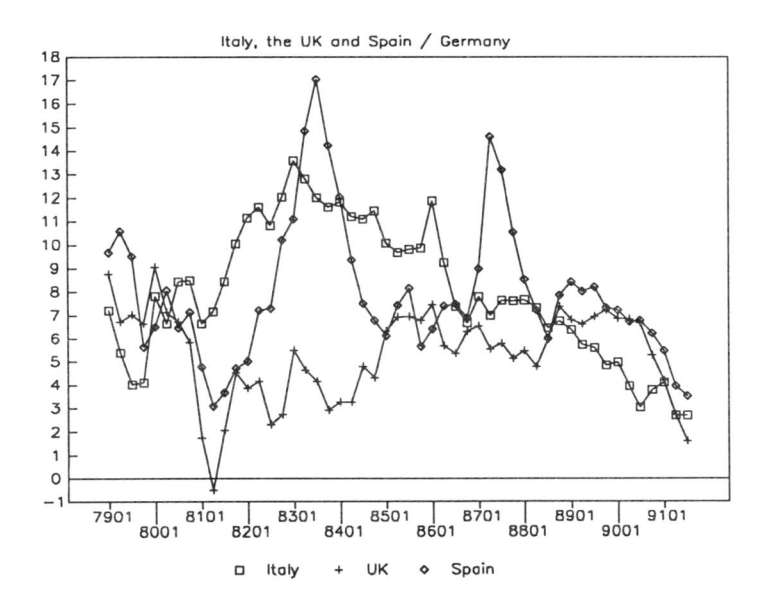

Chart 5b *Short-term interest differentials for Italy, the UK and Spain vis-a-vis Germany*

122 *Achieving Monetary Union in Europe*

Chart 5c *Short-term interest differentials for France, Belgium and Ireland vis-a-vis Germany*

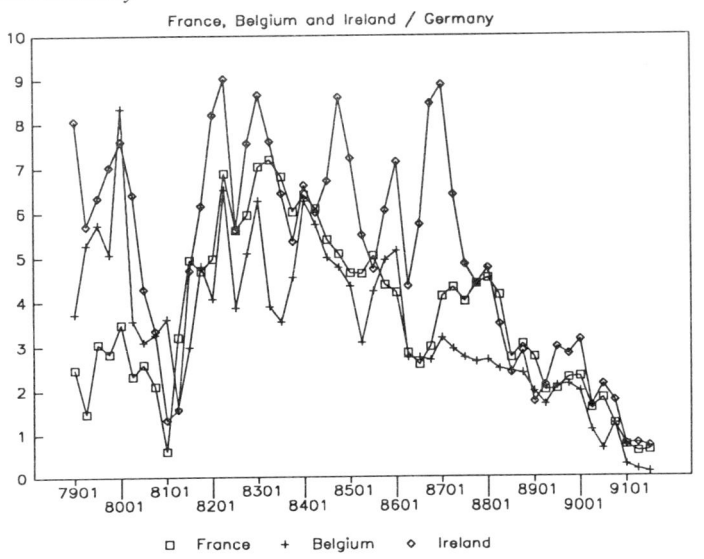

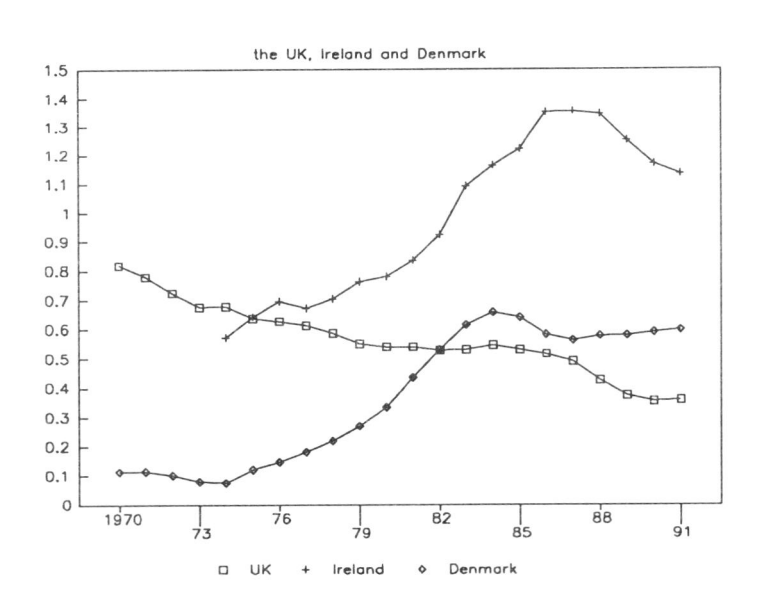

Chart 6a *Gross government debt to GDP ratios for the UK, Ireland and Denmark*

Chart 6b *Gross government debt to GDP ratios for Italy, the Netherlands and Belgium*

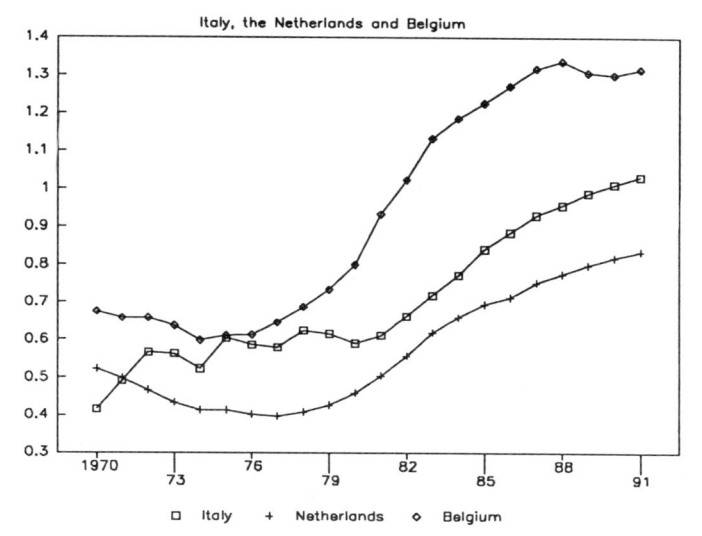

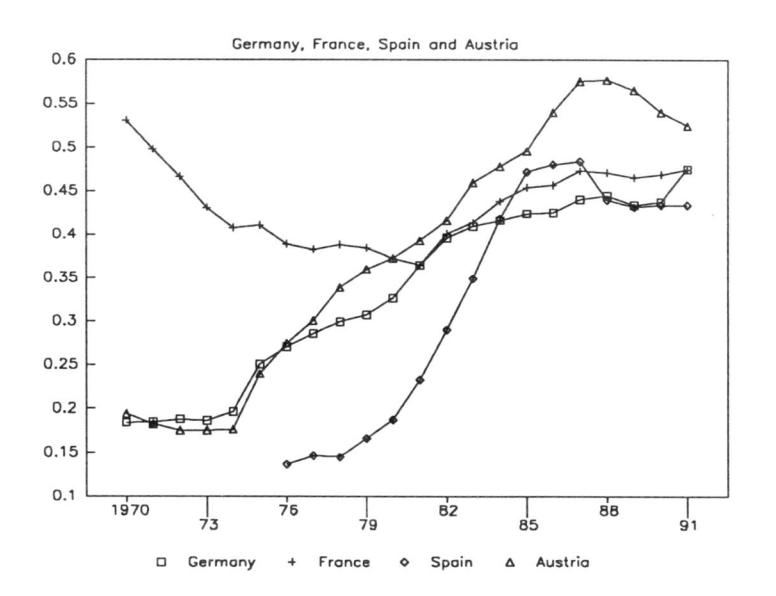

Chart 6c *Gross government debt to GDP ratios for Germany, France, Spain and Austria*

124 *Achieving Monetary Union in Europe*

Chart 7a *Current balance to GDP ratios for Germany, France and the Netherlands (current balance as % of GDP)*

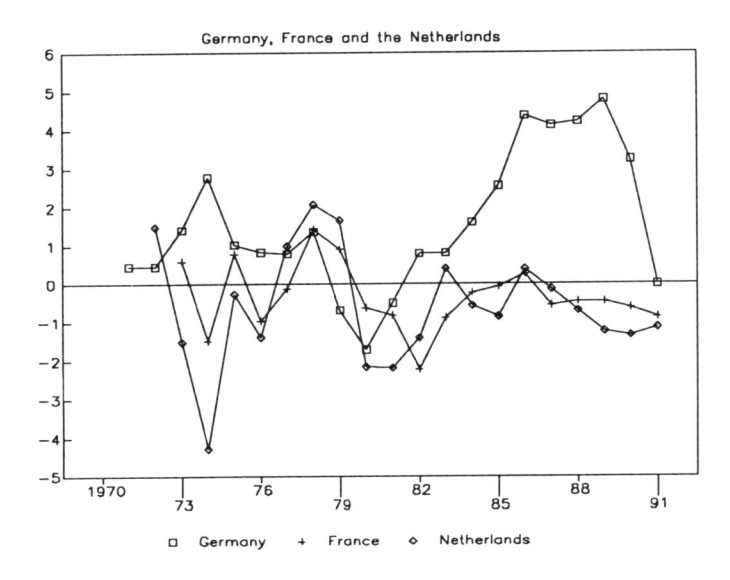

Chart 7b *Current balance to GDP ratios for Austria, Belgium, Denmark and Ireland (current balance as % of GDP)*

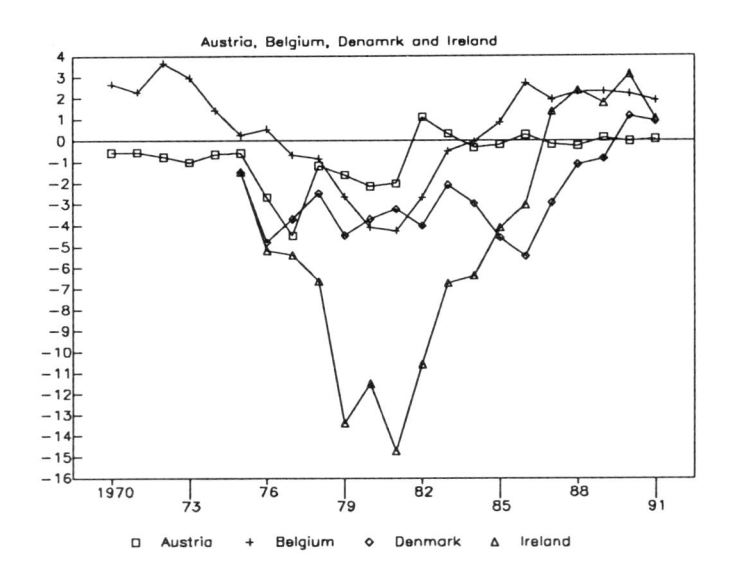

Chart 7c *Current balance to GDP ratios for Italy, Spain and the UK (current balance as % of GDP)*

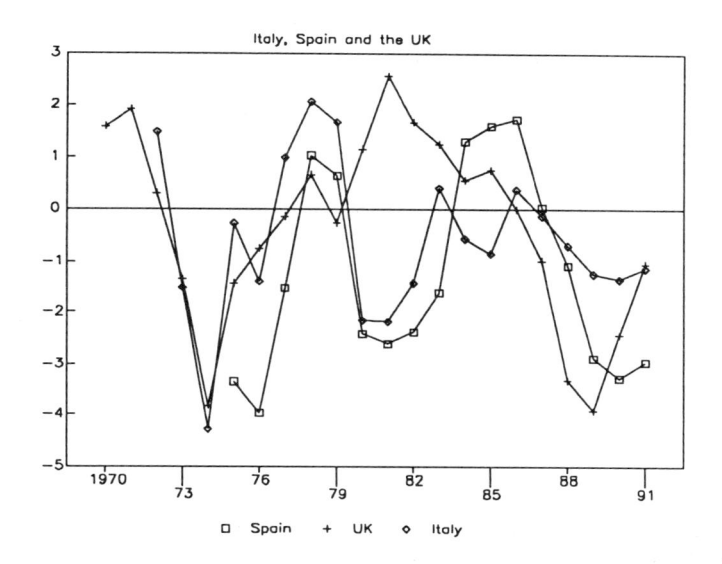

Sources: *Chart 1 to 7 NIESR database and Datastream.*

8

Microeconomic Conditions for Monetary Union

The sources of gain from monetary union at the microeconomic level are obvious and have been well articulated in *One market, one money*, by the European Commission. For anyone undertaking transactions with other member states in the Community, whether as an individual or a firm, there is likely to be a fall in cost and a reduction in uncertainty. However, the extent to which these potential gains will be translated into actual benefits, particularly for the firm, in terms of increased sales or profits, will depend upon the nature of the reactions to the changes agreed at Maastricht. Monetary union is very much part and parcel of European union as a whole and is one of the facilitating mechanisms for allowing the Community to reap the full benefits from the completion of the internal market. In this chapter we explore the nature of the changes which will need to take place at the microeconomic level for all organisations, whether commercial firms, public authorities, or financial intermediaries and for individuals, if the transition to monetary union is to be successful and the potential benefits are to be realised once Stage 3 takes effect.

The impact of EMU is not one sided. It also involves costs. In the process of transition, as firms and regions are opened to more competition from within the Community, some will lose, even though the market as a whole is likely to grow, as a result of the increased efficiency from removing unnecessary barriers and transactions costs. In that process no doubt some jobs will be lost. Unfortunately, if the line of argument advanced in *The Costs of non-Europe* is correct, the chances are that the net effect on employment may be negative initially, as the efficiency gains are implemented, before becoming positive as the results of the ensuing expansion of demand, both in Europe and markets elsewhere, stemming from the improved European competitiveness, has its effect. In the process of implementing a single currency, there are direct costs, from changing computer systems, producing new price lists and altering coin-operated machines, for example. Some firms will find they get more than offsetting gains from other aspects of the process but others will not.

The exact distribution of these gains and losses is not predetermined. It will depend on the responses of firms, employees, national regulatory authorities, households and other organisations in the Community to the changes in the framework of operation entailed by the Maastricht Treaty and the other legislation already being implemented for the 'completion' of the internal market. The legislative changes do not merely compel changes in behaviour, they also provide the opportunity for behaviour to change. It is up to those involved to decide how they wish to respond, both individually and collectively. While governments and the Community can do much by setting the macroeconomic conditions for EMU, the microeconomic response makes a major contribution both to the ease of the transition and the ultimate competitive success of the union.

The immediate microeconomic considerations from monetary union

It is not until the single currency is actually in place that firms can finally avoid having to pay foreign exchange transactions costs. Even in a Stage 3 of fixed exchange rates the extra transaction of exchange has to take place, although this may have a very small cost. In the first few years of the transition to EMU the major gains will come from the reduction in uncertainty as there is increasing convergence in the rate of price inflation among the member states. With similar rates of inflation the chance of exchange rates changing is greatly reduced. Hence, the expected future costs or income in domestic currency of transactions denominated in foreign currency become largely predictable. Under these circumstances pricing abroad within the Community becomes much more similar for the firm to pricing at home and the need to take out some form of insurance against loss from exchange rate variation, say in the form of options, is reduced. This does not of course imply that transactions within the forward foreign exchange market will cease to be important. The margin of variation would have to be less than that of the cost of the transaction for that to be true and that is unlikely before Stage 3.

The reduction in uncertainty not merely reduces costs of undertaking business in other member states, thereby enabling firms to quote a more competitive price, but increases their willingness to do so. Assuming the process of convergence is progressive then this will stimulate both trade and investment across the borders of member states progressively as we move through the stages of EMU. However, although increasing policy coordination among the member states should mean that their cyclical behaviour also becomes more coordinated, there is always the possibility that some of the shocks will have a sufficiently asymmetric effect that prices will diverge for a while, putting exchange rates under pressure as a consequence. Exchange risk is not eliminated.

As convergence of inflation rates proceeds, a second consequence for those countries which had higher rates of inflation is that interest rate differentials will also begin to fall. Large multinational companies are already able to exploit this differential by borrowing in the lower interest rate markets. These lower interest rates will result in some stimulus to investment and also to domestic consumer demand for durable goods. To some extent this will merely restore some of the imbalance caused by the need of the higher inflation countries to have a harsher monetary policy to reduce inflation in the first place. However, it is widely argued that this fall in interest rates will generate a dynamic gain to firms because their new investment will tend to be more productive and operate at lower unit costs than existing capital stock. This new plant and equipment will tend to embody the latest technology and will also enable the production of more advanced and higher quality products, all of which will contribute to increased competitiveness, sales and profitability, so that the process can be repeated.

The wider framework of change

These gains, through lower interest rates and exchange costs, only form part of the process of transformation for firms in the approach to EMU. The main sources of gain through the completion of the single market are well-known (see Mayes, *et al.*, 1991, for example). The removal of barriers at the frontier and to transport make trading easier and cheaper, the harmonisation of standards and the mutual recognition of testing will increase the effective size of markets for the sale of goods, hence enabling the exploitation of economies of scale where these are available. The recognition of qualifications and the right to establishment will enable firms to set up and supply services in other markets. However, the integration of goods markets is far more advanced than that of capital, labour and services markets, because such trade forms the traditional mechanism of bringing markets together. The quantitative and tariff barriers to trade in goods were abolished within the Community over twenty years ago.

In many respects it is these new areas which are most crucial in the success of EMU. Unless capital and labour can be fully mobile there will be continuing division of markets and failure to exploit the full range of gains available. This has two sets of microeconomic consequences. In the first place some firms will be unable to reorganise on a basis which would enable them to compete on more equal terms with their competitors from countries outside the EC. In the second, the gains will be very inequitably distributed and those in the less-favoured regions will find it difficult to compete. In part the solution to these difficulties lies within the scope of firms themselves. However, many of the difficulties occur because of the differences in the way in which the markets in the various member states operate.

Microeconomic Conditions for Monetary Union 129

To take two examples, on the one hand, inflationary pressures are in part generated by the way the wage bargaining system operates and, on the other, the reorganisation of business is inhibited by the structure of capital markets and the structure of property rights. In the former case, if management and workforce in one member state are able to negotiate wage deals which absorb a larger proportion of any external shock to production costs, then they are able to earn a competitive advantage. At present, much of the comparison made during bargaining is between firms within the same member state, thereby reinforcing the differences in performance. Achieving convergence with a lower unemployment cost in the more inflation- prone countries requires that the bargaining process pays attention to the behaviour of the least inflationary parts of the Community. In part, achieving this comparability is hampered by differences in bargaining systems. Where bargaining has a large element of economy-wide consensus to it, it may be possible to come to an agreement which holds inflation down more readily, because most people feel they have been fairly treated. Strong competition in a particular market may also result in lower settlements. It is not so much that one system is better than another but, because the markets operate according to different traditions, they produce different outcomes, lessening the degree to which the union represents a 'single' market.

The same sorts of problems apply in capital markets. The well known debate about the difference between German and British capital markets (described in Hart, 1991, for example) suggests that purchase of German firms on the market is rather more difficult than in the Netherlands or the UK. The role of the major banks as shareholders and as the holders of proxies for other shareholders in Germany is thought to contribute to this difference. Associated with this is the suggestion that institutional shareholders in the UK take a shorter-run view of the necessary returns on their equity investments. These sorts of differences between the structures in member states tend to maintain the fragmentation of the market. If one approach is clearly inferior to another then, as the market opens, this will become apparent.

The previous barriers have restricted competition between regimes. With the removal of the barriers the regime differences will tend to be eroded or polarised but it is not clear what sort of evolutionary process will occur to achieve this result. One or more of the regimes which prevail in an existing member state may come to dominate the system. An example of this comes from the role of the central bank in EMU. The German system has proved to be effective in providing a control for inflation. Therefore, many of the key features of the German system have been incorporated into the Maastricht Treaty. As set out in Shipman and Mayes (1991), there is no need for the new rules to be established by an external authority. The operation of the market itself can achieve the change. This can be seen very clearly with the way that some of the methods which are thought to have contributed to the success of Japanese companies — just-in-time manufacturing, methods of quality management, and so on — have been adopted by other companies in Europe and America. The European Union agreed at Maastricht offers the opportunity for the best of European methods to diffuse through the Community as a whole.

The new treaty has recognised areas where activity by individual firms in assisting the process of transition may be relatively difficult in the absence of an appropriate framework, one of the most important of which is vocational training. The reform of the structural funds in 1988 already recognised that vocational training for the unemployed needed to come through intervention by the public sector. It further recognised that the existence of underutilised resources on this scale was a Community problem rather than just a national or regional one. The Maastricht agreement emphasises the role of vocational training. However, it is not just the unemployed for whom the problem applies if Europe is aiming to compete on the basis of strength in knowledge-based industries. Training within the firm needs to be a continuing activity. Without a framework where all firms are involved in such training there is a temptation for those which have not provided the training to poach employees from the others. This in turn discourages the other firms from providing the training either as they fear they will lose the people they have just trained.

Implementing the single currency

Many of the gains from monetary union occur progressively as inflation rates fall and exchange-rate variations become smaller. However, the full range of gains only occurs when the single currency itself is introduced. Although Stage 3 of EMU involves the permanent fixing of exchange rates and the introduction of the ecu as the single currency of Europe, it is not clear whether it is intended that the single currency would be introduced on day one or after some further period of transition. A firm's strategy in responding to EMU therefore also needs to include a transition path.

If it were the case that current circumstances were to be maintained up to E-day, when the ecu is introduced, replacing the existing currencies, and that the timetable for that introduction were fixed and known, firms would be able to set out a fairly straightforward set of plans for handling the transition and try to make sure that they maximised the benefits available to them. As it is the transition is both gradual and of uncertain pace. Let us begin, however, by considering the changes required for the full Stage 3, including the single currency, and return to the problems of the path of integration later.

For most firms changing to a single currency will mean that they will have to alter their pricing systems, both internally and externally, their invoicing and their payments — both to suppliers and employees. The

Microeconomic Conditions for Monetary Union 131

operations of their treasury department will change and there will be some problems for the alteration in the valuation of their assets and liabilities. For small firms with little exposure to foreign transactions the changes will be relatively straightforward. The exchange rate between their domestic currency and the ecu would have already been established. If the ecu is introduced after the start of Stage 3, so that exchange rates are completely fixed, there will not even be marginal fluctuations to worry about in the last stages of the transition. The main change, therefore, as far as financial systems will be concerned, is that all values will have to be multiplied by the conversion factor.

Thus, to take what will probably be the simplest example, if the D-Mark still has its current central rate against the ecu of 2.05586 on the date of adoption of the ecu, then to express all D-Mark values henceforward in ecu would involve dividing them by 2.05586 (multiplying by 1/2.05586). The fact that this factor has five decimal places is no problem for a computer but it would strain the capacities for most people's mental arithmetic. Not surprisingly there is some pressure to round these numbers in the final fixing of exchange rates, at least to the smallest whole currency unit in use. However, for most transactions this is not really a problem. Conversion charts would be produced for everyone in the country so that they can compute any specific change. For goods in the shops prices would be printed in both currencies for a transition period both before and after E-day.

Since the D-Mark ceases operation one day and is replaced by the ecu the next there is no real need to convert from one currency to the other except on E-day itself. The main problem is for people to change their frame of reference, so that they get used to comparing relative prices in ecu and that they can be sure that the change in currency has not been used as a covert excuse to raise prices. (Clearly there has to be a 'rounding rule' otherwise there is scope for some to profit from the addition of large numbers of the fractions of the smallest unit involved in the transactions.) A similar familiarisation process will be necessary for the new notes and coins but there is widespread experience of the means of doing this, both from wholesale changes in the currency, like decimalisation in the UK and German monetary union.

Thus for most firms it will be a matter of running the appropriate computer package for their accounting, invoicing and payments systems overnight on E-day. The bigger the firm, the more complex that operation, and for banks the sheer conversion is likely to take a few days and as a consequence we can expect that E-day will be accompanied by a long weekend of bank closure, perhaps four or five days. There will also be a difficult period of transition when the notes and coin in circulation are changed but experience suggests that even though an extended period may be available that most people choose to change over as quickly as possible. The bulk of these problems will be encountered by the retail sector and others who handle cash. For most firms transactions are undertaken by cheque or by other bank instrument so the problem will be small.

These changes are not likely to take place before 1997 so there is plenty of time to prepare. Since this will be a potential source of profit for firms involved in providing the transition mechanisms, like the computer software companies, accountancy firms and the banks themselves, we can expect that there will be considerable competition to provide the necessary assistance with the transition. The physical changes that need to be made to tills and coin machines are also a common and predictable problem, which can be planned for. Modern electronic designs have actually equipped such machines for change. Since all the member states have decimal currencies the nature of the change will be largely trivial. Those whose computerised systems or machines cannot readily be changed will tend to incur larger costs and inconvenience — an incentive to invest.

The transition itself and the uncertainty about its timing and length pose some dilemmas for firms. Financial intermediaries face a wide range of problems during the transition and in setting up the new systems for EMU. Levitt (1991) discusses some of the problems involved in setting up ecu payments systems. In an ideal world banking in EMU would operate throughout the Community in ecu in the same way that it does within each member state in their own currency at present. In this way cheques written in any part of the Community could be quickly and cheaply cleared for payment. There are several ways in which this might occur. A completely new system could be set up. There could be a network of linked national systems. In the spirit of a competitive market there is no reason why there should not be more than one system operating in parallel. However, there will need to be some agreement over their structure as some sorts of systems are not compatible. Central banks and the EMI will no doubt wish to be involved in these discussions but the form of the agreement needs to occur earlier rather than later in the process.

As Stage 3 approaches, the difference between costs of transactions between currencies and those in a single currency will become a matter of increasing concern. It could be countered by an explicit agreement on charging to try to overcome this form of implicit discrimination. In a Stage 3 of fixed exchange rates but before the introduction of the single currency many of the complications of the current separation of national systems will continue to apply. The role of the ecu in the transition also affects the way the system might operate. If its role is to be deliberately increased, then transaction costs involving it may be reduced relative to other foreign exchange transactions and the profile of the transition from using a variety of foreign currencies to the eventual use of the ecu alone will be progressive rather than occurring as a single step change on E-day.

Firms are therefore faced by a dilemma. Should they postpone all change to the last possible moment or will it make sense to introduce some of the new procedures at an earlier stage? De Monceau (1991) identifies one area where multinational companies might wish to change earlier. For their internal transactions and accounting they need ultimately to express everything in a single currency. The most obvious choice at present is the domestic currency of the country in which they have to report and pay taxes, although, for those involved primarily in activities involving commodities denominated in dollars, such as oil, the dollar might be more appropriate. However, since the ecu will be the ultimate currency in which the transactions will take place, some organisations, like the Amadeus ticket and reservation system, for example, have decided from the outset to use the ecu as their common currency.

Some of these changes are progressive as Europe moves closer to Stage 3 and into the first part of Stage 3 itself, when exchange rates are fixed but the single currency is yet to be implemented. Others are step changes occurring at E-day or when Stage 3 starts. Thus far we have focussed on transactions but firms will also have to consider the development of the structure of their assets. Contracts taken out in ecu up till now may have to be re-expressed if they fall due for repayment after E-day with only some of the ingredient currencies of the current ecu basket actually being a party to the single currency. A profile of changes can therefore be set against the timetable of the official stages of EMU and the actual convergence of the member states.

Focussing on financial changes alone, however, will be insufficient as the convergence of economic policies, regulatory regimes and structures affects the degree to which companies can treat the growing union as a single market. At present the Community is embarked on a process of regime competition among the policies of the Community, the member states and even regions. It is still debated where the differences among regimes constitute discrimination in favour of domestic companies, say, through cross-share holdings, which may restrict entry and exit. This is being resolved in areas such as state aids where all such intervention outside the less favoured regions is thought likely to discriminate. Regulatory regimes may have no such discriminatory intent and while deregulation may be the easiest means of achieving equal treatment among the member states it is not necessarily optimal for the wider public interest.

Hence in the transition period we can expect that there will be movements of activity towards member states and currencies where the treatment seems to be favourable. However, national and Community administrations will not sit by on the sidelines and will react as they see results occurring which they regard as inequitable. One area where this is happening most obviously at present is in the realm of competition policy. Not only is there debate among the member states about whether each others' policies are fairly applied but there is debate about the conflict between the Commission's judgement and that of member states and also about the difference between the Commission's view and global competition with the policies applied in the US, Japan and elsewhere.

The resolution of the regimes and the variety of behaviour across the Community will all form part of the process of microeconomic convergence towards EMU. Uniformity is unlikely to be the result in most areas as the aspects of the competitive process tend to foster diversity and innovation but competition among regimes will tend to lead to changes in those which have a substantially adverse effect on competitiveness. There have been no serious attempts to forecast how long this process of evolution will take. The stages of EMU and the single market programme will expose an increasingly wide range of activities to competition but it is highly unlikely that many differences will have been resolved by the time the single currency is implemented.

9

The Timetable

The agreement at Maastricht sets a steady timetable for reaching EMU, which follows on that of the single market. So that we have

1st January 1993:
    single market measures to come into effect*
    European Union Treaty takes effect
before the end of 1993:
    cohesion fund set up
1st January 1994:
    Stage 2 of Monetary Union
        European Monetary Institute begins operation
        Monetary Committee begins operation
before end 1996:
    decision on whether to go ahead on Stage 3
    and on who qualifies
1st January 1997:
    possible starting date for Stage 3
        Components of Stage 3
            European Central Bank takes over from EMI
            Economic and Financial Committee takes over from Monetary Committee
            and, at a date to be fixed,
        ecu becomes the single currency of Europe
before 1st July 1998:
    decision on who shall qualify for Stage 3
1st January 1999:
    last possible date for start of Stage 3

*some of these measures will be phased in later in the decade and others are still to be agreed.

During 1992, negotiations on the membership of Austria, Sweden and probably Finland are likely to begin. Assuming they are successful, these three countries would join the Community within a year or two and would be fully involved in the process of transition to EMU. Ideally they should join in time for the start of Stage 2 but that would be a very rapid timetable.

Another crucial step in the timetable is the agreement of the five-year budgetary perspective for 1993-8, which will take place during 1992. This will decide the scale and relative priorities assigned to various of the policies designed to ease the process of convergence.

Acheiving the timetable

In the earlier chapters we have discussed what has to be done by the Community, governments of member states, central banks, other financial institutions, commercial companies and the ordinary citizen, during the period of transition and into the final Stage 3 if EMU is to be achieved. From the microeconomic point of view the time required to organise the implementation of the single currency, the payments and other systems for banks and the invoicing, pricing and payments systems for commercial firms, *including the associated training* to make sure it runs properly — even the alteration of physical equipment like ticket machines and automatic tellers — is actually quite short. Surveys of firms and financial institutions suggest that they would like about three to four years for the change. Experience from other changes in currency systems, like German monetary unification and decimalisation in the UK, suggests that these changes can be achieved even more rapidly, should the need arise, perhaps in as little as two years for most companies. The ones who need the greatest lead in times are the computer software companies who have to organise the new systems and the changeover packages which have to be implemented at E-day.

Other physical changes like minting the new currency and printing the new notes also require considerable effort beyond normal capacity but again that can be planned as, for example, a mint can be constructed in less than a year. There are fears that it will take some time after E-day for many people to adjust to the new system but again the experience of other changes suggests that if the population in general is well briefed, with specimen coinage sets available well beforehand, with, for example, dual pricing in the shops for six months or so to acclimatise people to the new value system and reassure them that they were not being overcharged, then most adjust within days rather than weeks. Special efforts have to be made for small firms, who will tend to postpone any action as long as possible, because it involves extra expenditure and effort. Assessments of the costs to firms, banks and individuals suggest that these are not of a dimension that cannot be coped with by the system as a whole and that no system of compensation will be necessary. However, provisions for easing and encouraging transition are likely to be implemented by the Community, the member states and local organisations, including chambers of commerce. Given the structure planned for EMU under the Maastricht agreement there are no real microeconomic problems in arranging implementation by 1997 still less by 1999, if the process starts soon. The technical side of the macroeconomic arrangements will also take some time to set up but a five-year run-in should give more than enough time to establish the procedures and iron out the difficulties. The interim arrangements with the EMI and the Monetary Committee will give a lot of the necessary experience in coordination.

The apparent neatness of this arrangement is disturbed by the fact that we do not know either the date of starting Stage 3 or which countries will be participating at the beginning. We have also talked as if the ecu will be introduced on day one. The actual date for introduction is not spelt out and one could easily see the ECB wanting to take Stage 3 in two steps, digesting the operation of a single monetary policy and the cooperation of the member central banks first and then introducing the ecu once procedures are established. The Treaty provisions do, however, entail that the sequence cannot be reversed; the single currency cannot precede the ECB.

The existence of this range of possibilities causes non-trivial problems, because companies are reluctant to act under uncertainty. They incur costs in the transition and have far less tangible expectations of the gains. The tangible gains come when they can eliminate currency risk, and reduce their transactions costs. Much of this occurs either after E-day or at least in the final rundown, when the date of Stage 3 is known and not far off. Companies in or dealing extensively with member states which might not be successful in meeting the criteria for convergence by any particular date will be faced with the greatest problems. They may have to continue with multicurrency systems. They will have costs from what they do have to change but will not be able to eliminate systems to be able to get the full cost savings. They will still be faced by a degree of exchange uncertainty and higher interest rates.

Certainty will only be introduced for some countries very late on in the day. For example, the Council only has to decide by July 1998 who will be admitted to Stage 3 at the beginning of 1999. That gives firms only perhaps six months to adjust. It could be argued that everybody can read the macroeconomic indicators and hence can get a longer lead in time for the non-marginal cases. However, that still does not get over the problem that the date of commencement before the 1999 deadline is not fixed, nor is the date of decision, apart from the need to have a first attempt before the end of 1996. It also does not get round the problem that there is a suspicion that convergence conditions may be varied when it comes close to making a decision which would have to exclude 'core' countries under a rigid application of the criteria. Again this increases uncertainty.

It is clear from our discussions in Chapter 7, that it is our impression that all member states, with the exception of Greece, have the potential to achieve the preconditions for entering Stage 3, provided that they are interpreted with a little licence. As the actual outcome will be the upshot of a combination of economic reactions, political will and external shocks, there is clearly also ample opportunity to fail. This convergence also requires adequate cohesion and our conclusions presuppose that the cohesion fund and the expansion of the various approaches towards tackling the problems of less favoured regions are actually implemented.

The largest question marks hang over Portugal, Spain and Italy. The UK of course has a self-imposed question mark in that it has to take an explicit decision whether to join if it meets the convergence criteria. We have already expressed our view that in those circumstances the UK is likely to join if the large majority of the member states have converged. It is also our view that there is unlikely to be much difference in the decision-making whether it is made in 1996 or 1998 except for the marginal cases. Extending by an extra two years may actually result in some member states not converging on the second occasion although they did on the first, because of the risks of shocks and the political difficulty of sustaining tight policies in the absence of the external framework of Stage 3 to compel it.

It is, thus, clear from our discussions that we expect that at least one country will not be able to participate in Stage 3 at the outset and as many as six could plausibly fail to close the gap or choose not to participate even by 1999. We therefore have to consider the question of how a partial system might work. In any case there have to be mechanisms for new members of the EC to make a transition to full EMU and indeed some extension of the EMS, including the ERM, to accommodate this second group of countries, some of which might be associates rather than full member states.

A partial EMU

In purely technical terms the position of the excluded member states is quite clear. Arrangements have been made for them to have derogations from various obligations and the UK in particular has a specific list of obligations that shall not apply if it decides not to participate in Stage 3. In effect all the objectives of economic policy apply, in that price stability is still an aim and that all the provisions of good economic management are required. The monitoring role will still apply and the member state will receive opinions on how it should act. The difference is that there are no sanctions for failure to comply — except of course that this will mean that convergence conditions are unlikely to be achieved. The ECB will have no jurisdiction over the central banks of excluded member states and they will have no role in appointing the members of the Executive Board and will not be participating in the Governing Council. The ECB will, however, set the rules over their holdings of ecus as they will for any other external holders.

Thus up to the start of Stage 3 all member states are part of the full system of the Monetary Committee and the EMI but once Stage 3 starts only those who are accepted will continue with full participation. There are thus problems for those who are excluded. They lose their say in policy and they do not gain the cost advantages of the single currency. There is no statement about what happens to other aspects of policy such as the use of cohesion funds so those continue to apply, but management of an external exchange rate with a close parity in the transition for an excluded member state will become more difficult than for member states as a whole in Stage 2, when there will be a much more reciprocal basis of intervention and assistance.

The excluded member states would presumably be within some form of EMS, with a version of the ERM being used for those that were further advanced in the process of convergence. Since the ecu would be a currency in its own right they would have an exchange rate with it and their currencies would not form a component of it as at present. The ERM would thus come closer to the idea of the snake in some respects. Periodic realignments could be expected for some of the currencies, particularly those new to the system, so for those currencies the arrangement might look rather more like the 'soft' EMS of the period before 1987. Obviously for a currency on the threshold of admission to Stage 3, the relationship with respect to the ecu would be very stable.

There is always the danger that such a flexible system might regress if it exhibits a lot of realignment and loses credibility as the snake did. There is thus a very considerable incentive to be in the system from the outset. Not only will the credibility of a country which has failed to converge be weakened, raising its interest rates, but it will suffer a relative loss from higher transactions costs with its trading partners within the EC. It is also not a party to the decision-making about whether it should be admitted to Stage 3 at a subsequent date. Thus to some extent convergence to membership of Stage 3 becomes harder for existing member states once Stage 3 starts. New member states, on the other hand, have no worsening of their position and the transition, even though it is a one-sided process, is no more difficult than shadowing the ecu would be from the outside, with all the added benefits from other Community policies.

It is thus readily possible to run a multispeed system, with member states being full participants in the single market but not part of Stage 3 of EMU. Such a lack of participation will mean inevitably that they are less integrated as transactions costs with them will be higher. However, they will be free to use the exchange rate as a means of achieving convergence if they find that this reduces the costs to the economy as a whole.

The exchange rate is only a part of transactions costs of firms. There will not be equality of transactions costs even within EMU as those organisations which are more peripherally located, smaller, higher risk, and so on will still pay a premium. Thus not being part of Stage 3 may only impose a relatively small cost on those in excluded member states. It will, however, have a somewhat asymmetric effect on financial markets. Foreign exchange markets will be more important for excluded member states and ecu markets less important, which may affect the ability of their financial institutions to compete.

The existence of an alternative status in the EC from not being within Stage 3 and the treatment of the social chapter in the Treaty, where, in effect, countries can choose whether they wish to participate in a particular area of policy, open the door to a Community where the degree of integration can vary quite considerably among the member states. Whether this is a unifying or weakening force will depend on its operation. If excluded member states are shown to be prospering because of their lack of participation in particular areas of integration, then this will encourage others to join them and could reverse some of the integration process. On the other hand, an increase in flexibility permits states with wider divergences to continue to be part of the system. Thus, although the degree of economic integration might be lower if flexibility is permitted, this arrangement may greatly improve the stability and durability of the Community as a whole.

Permitting more variation in the degree of integration will help in laying a path for lower income states to enter the Community gradually, slowly integrating towards closer union, rather than having to agree on accession to move directly towards complete union according to a preordained timetable. Since the existing member states will not stand still, either in terms of GDP/head or in the extent of their integration, gaps between them and aspiring applicants will, at best, only close slowly, even if other policies of assistance are relatively successful. If these aspirants are not to be excluded for the indefinite future by the existence of these gaps, then a more flexible method of entry is required. The provisions in the Maastricht Treaty offer that way forward.

It is hence an empirical matter whether this flexibility turns out to be a unifying force. The real test will be adverse external economic circumstances. Exclusion from Stage 3 gives member state governments the appearance of having more freedom to instigate policies intended to mitigate those adverse conditions. Exclusion from the social chapter may also offer temporary competitiveness advantages by permitting a less generous level of social provision while the country is trying to converge to meet the preconditions for joining Stage 3. Clearly this process of opting in and out of EC policy areas cannot readily be extended far, otherwise member states would be able to choose to participate in the beneficial parts of the single market and EMU while avoiding some of the costs, thereby free riding on the full participants. This does not seem to be a plausible basis for agreement. The degree to which partial participation can be accepted is bound to be limited but the position of the EFTA states, participating in much of the single market but not in EMU, looks like the current limit to the exercise. Here we already see that two and probably three EFTA states do not find the idea of participation without representation within the system attractive. If others follow, this will be a very straightforward test of whether the Maastricht proposals will increase the unifying force of the Community in Europe.

Concluding remarks

In the foregoing analysis we have made it clear that we expect Austria (assuming it joins the Community by then), Belgium, Denmark, France, Germany, Luxembourg and the Netherlands to be agreed on being ready to move to Stage 3 of EMU at the beginning of 1997. We expect that all or most of Ireland, Italy, Spain, Sweden (assuming membership) and the United Kingdom will be in the same position but in these cases there is some qualification over the likelihood. Beyond these eleven countries, it is also possible that Portugal and Finland (if a member state) could be judged ready. The most serious question mark hangs over Greece, for whom meeting the full criteria for convergence is not feasible, to the extent that it seems unlikely that the other member states would be willing to accept that full participation is possible.

In our opinion, therefore, the odds are heavily on Stage 3 going ahead on 1 January 1997. Even if some of the second group of five countries are not quite ready then we would expect them to have joined within five years along with Finland. This prospect should be enough to obtain the unanimous agreement of the member states necessary on that occasion. If Greece and Portugal are not ready it will be clear that further exchange rate adjustment will be required before they can converge sufficiently. Delay in decision-making by a couple of years, from 1996 to 1988 for commencement in 1999 rather than 1997, is unlikely to alter the position much and it increases the chance that there will be adverse external economic shocks which might take some states away from convergence. The political cost of achieving convergence is also likely to be considerable in some parts of the Community and the longer this has to be sustained independently before being cemented into cooperation of the union, the greater the chance of wavering. This argues against waiting until 1998 in the hope that circumstances might improve.

We hope therefore that the Community will rapidly come to the conclusion that 1 January 1997 is *the* date and make that clear to all both inside and outside the Community. It was very clear from the research undertaken for *A Strategy for the ECU* that if firms are to act in time to implement the single currency smoothly and at a reasonable cost a fixed, feasible and relatively short timetable needs to be established. 1999 is beyond the usual planning horizon. Credibility is a key ingredient for success as durable convergence in the Community involves a change in inflation expectations. The uncertainties of previous attempts at EMU demonstrate the risks but the remarkable success of the 1992 programme in transforming expectations shows that a well executed strategy can succeed even if it might appear ambitious.

This strategy needs to include a date for the introduction of the ecu as the single currency. Our clear preference was for this to coincide with the start of Stage 3 but from the terms of the Treaty a swift transition seems to be expected, so a date during 1997 would appear suitable. The opportunity for setting these targets and the timetable now exists with the negotiation over the new five-year budgetary perspective for 1993-8. This could be the 'Budget for European Union' offering the necessary cohesion offering the necessary support for the Community to move forward together in the spirit of the Treaty agreed at Maastricht. 1992 will thus be doubly a key year, marking the 'completion' of the internal market programme and the start of a new timetable to EMU before the end of the decade. The decision has to be made. We hope this book will assist it.

References

Aitken, N.D. (1973), 'The effect of the EEC and EFTA on European trade: temporal cross-section analysis', *American Economic Review*, vol. 63, no.5, December.

Anderton, R., Barrell, R. and in't Veld, J.W. (1992), 'Macroeconomic convergence in Europe: achievements and prospects' in Barrell, R. (ed), *op.cit.*

AUME (1990), *A Strategy for the ECU*, report prepared by Ernst & Young and the National Institute of Economic and Social Research, London, Kogan Page.

Baer, G.D. and Padoa-Schioppa, T. (1989), 'The Werner Report revisited', in (Delors) *Report on Economic and Monetary Union in the Community*, pp.53-60.

Barrell, R. (ed) (1992), *Economic Convergence and Monetary Union in Europe*, London, Sage Publications.

Bordes, C. and Girardin, E. (1992), 'The achievements of the ERM and the preconditions for monetary union: a French perspective', in Barrell, R. (ed), *op.cit.*

Bradley, J. and Whelan, K. (1992), 'Irish experience of monetary linkages with the United Kingdom and developments since joining the EMS' in Barrell, R. (ed), *op.cit.*

Brooks, S.J. (1979), 'The experience of floating exchange rates' in Major, R.L.M. (ed), *Britain's Trade and Exchange Rate Policy*, London, Heinemann.

Carmagni, R. (ed) (1991), *Innovation Networks*, London, Belhaven Press.

Collignon, S. (1992), 'An ecu zone for central and eastern Europe: a supportive framework for convergence' in Barrell, R. (1992), *op.cit.*

De Monceau, C. (1991),Speech to the European Finance Convention, Amsterdam, November.

El Agraa, A.M. (ed) (1985), *The Economics of the European Community*, Oxford, Philip Allan.

Franzmeyer, F. et al. (1991), 'The regional impact of Community policies', European Parliament Research and Documentation Paper no. 17.

Friedman, W. (1992), 'German monetary union and some lessons for Europe' in Barrell, R. (ed), *op.cit.*

Gros, D. and Thygesen, N. (1988), 'The EMS: achievements, current issues and directions for the future', CEPS Paper no. 35, March.

Hart, P.E. (1991), `Internal and external growth in British and German companies', National Institute of Economic and Social Research Working Paper.

Hingel, A. (1991), 'Archipelago Europe - islands of innovation', CEC, Monitor/FAST prospective dossier, No. 1, April.

House of Lords (1992), *EEC Regional Development Policy*, 4th report of the Select Committee on The European Communities, HL20, London, HMSO.

in't Veld, J.W. (1992), 'The diverse experience of the Netherlands, Belgium and Denmark in the ERM' in Barrell, R. (ed), *op.cit.*

Kaldor, N. (1971), 'The truth about the dynamic effects', *New Statesman*, 12 March.
Kay, J.A. and Posner, M.V. (1989), 'Routes to economic integration. 1992 in the European Community', *National Institute Economic Review*, no. 129, pp.55-68.
Langfeldt, E. (1992), 'European Monetary Union: design and implementation' in Barrell, R. (ed), *op.cit.*
Levitt, M. (1991), 'Future European payments systems', National Institute of Economic and Social Research Briefing Note no. 1.
MacDougall, D. (1977), *Report of the Study Group on the role of public finance in European integration*, Brussels, European Commission.
Mayes, D.G. et al. (1991), *The European Challenge: industry's response to the 1992 programme*, London, Harvester-Wheatsheaf.
Mayes, D.G. et al. (1992), *The External Implications of European Integration*, proceedings of joint ESRC-ICS conference, London, Harvester-Wheatsheaf.
Nam, C.W. et al (1991), *The Effect of 1992 and Associated Legislation on the Less-favoured Regions of the Community*, European Parliament Research and Documentation Paper, no. 18.
National Institute of Economic and Social Research (1991), *A New Strategy for Social and Economic Cohesion after 1992*, European Parliament, Research and Documentation Paper, no. 19.
National Institute of Economic and Social Research (1992), *Single Europe Market Newsletter*, no. 1, January.
O'Donnell, R. (1991), 'Policy requirements for regional balance in economic and monetary union' in Hannequart, A., *Economic and Social Cohesion and the Structural Funds*, Routledge.
Onofri, P. and Tomasini, S. (1992), 'France and Italy: a tale of two adjustments' in Barrell, R. (ed), *op.cit.*
Padoa-Schioppa, T. (1987), *Efficiency, Stability and Equity: a Strategy for the Evolution of the Economic System of the European Community*, Oxford, Oxford University Press.
Pelkmans, J. (1984), *Market Integration in the European Community*, The Hague, Martinus Nijhoff.
Shipman, A. and Mayes, D.G. (1990), 'A framework for examining government and company responses to 1992', National Institute of Economic and Social Research Discussion Paper no. 199.
Wallace, W. (1991), *From Twelve to Twenty Four? The Challenges to the EC posed by the Revolutions in Eastern Europe*, Andrew Schonfield Association, Trinity College, Oxford.
Woolcock, S. (1990), 'US views of 1992', *National Institute Economic Review*, no. 134, November, pp. 86-92.